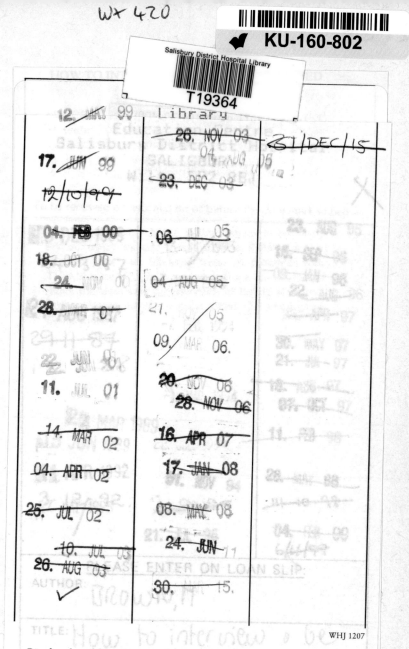

Salisbury District Hospital Library

Telephone: Salisbury (01722) 336262   extn. 4432 / 33
Out of hours answer machine in operation

Overcoming Common Problems Series

The ABC of Eating
Coping with anorexia, bulimia and
compulsive eating
JOY MELVILLE

Acne
How it's caused and how to cure it
PAUL VAN RIEL

An A–Z of Alternative Medicine
BRENT Q. HAFEN AND KATHRYN J.
FRANDSEN

Arthritis
Is your suffering really necessary?
DR WILLIAM FOX

Birth Over Thirty
SHEILA KITZINGER

Body Language
How to read others' thoughts by their gestures
ALLAN PEASE

Calm Down
How to cope with frustration and anger
DR PAUL HAUCK

Common Childhood Illnesses
DR PATRICIA GILBERT

Coping with Depression and Elation
DR PATRICK McKEON

Curing Arthritis–The Drug-free Way
MARGARET HILLS

Depression
DR PAUL HAUCK

Divorce and Separation
ANGELA WILLANS

Enjoying Motherhood
DR BRUCE PITT

The Epilepsy Handbook
SHELAGH McGOVERN

Everything You Need to know about Contact Lenses
DR ROBERT YOUNGSON

Everything You Need to know about Your Eyes
DR ROBERT YOUNGSON

Everything You Need to know about Shingles
DR ROBERT YOUNGSON

Family First Aid and Emergency Handbook
DR ANDREW STANWAY

Fears and Phobias
What they are and how to overcome them
DR TONY WHITEHEAD

Feverfew
A traditional herbal remedy for migraine and
arthritis
DR STEWART JOHNSON

Fight Your Phobia and Win
DAVID LEWIS

Fit Kit
DAVID LEWIS

Flying Without Fear
TESSA DUCKWORTH AND DAVID
MILLER

Goodbye Backache
DR DAVID IMRIE WITH COLLEEN
DIMSON

Guilt
Why it happens and how to overcome it
DR VERNON COLEMAN

How to Bring Up your Child Successfully
DR PAUL HAUCK

How to Control your Drinking
DRS MILLER AND MUNOZ

How to Cope with Stress
DR PETER TYRER

Overcoming Common Problems Series

Overcoming Common Problems Series

Overcoming Common Problems

HOW TO INTERVIEW AND BE INTERVIEWED

Michèle Brown
and Gyles Brandreth

SHELDON PRESS
LONDON

First published in Great Britain in 1986 by
Sheldon Press, SPCK, Marylebone Road, London NW1 4DU

British Library Cataloguing in Publication Data
Brown, Michèle
    How to interview and be interviewed.—
    (Overcoming common problems)
    1. Interviewing
    I. Title   II. Brandreth, Gyles   III. Series
    158'.3   BF637.15

    ISBN 0–85969–497–6
    ISBN 0–85969–498–4 Pbk

Typeset by Deltatype, Ellesmere Port, South Wirral
Printed in Great Britain by
Whitstable Litho Ltd, Whitstable, Kent

Contents

Acknowledgements

Barclays Bank plc
British Institute of Management
Christine Cox, National Extension College
Anne Crosby, CTVC
Janice Crosweller, Jobclub, Walthamstow
Gillian Edwards, Samurai Course manager, The Actors' Institute
Denia Evans, Plus Four Analysis Ltd
John Goss, Video Image Projection
Miss K. Harris, Professional and Executive Recruitment
Imperial College, London, Careers Advisory Office
The Industrial Society
Institute of Personnel Management
John Lidstone, Marketing Improvements Ltd
Miss Elizabeth Moon, Sales Director, Senior Secretaries
National Westminster Bank plc
David Robertson, Dean, and Fellow and Tutor in Politics, St
   Hugh's College, Oxford
David Rogers, public relations consultant
Susan Stoyell, Search-Write Stationery Company

Introduction

Skill as an interviewer or at being interviewed is quite separate from being able to do your own job—and it is a technique that can be learned.

There are professional personnel workers for whom the interview has developed into an art form, and there are many books available to help professional interviewers and selectors make accurate and informed decisions on whom to accept into their company's workforce. They have at their disposal tests, graphs, procedures, statistics and polls to help them sift through the applicants who come to their doors. This book does not presume to teach them anything. It is aimed at the vast majority of people, interviewers and interviewees, who have no training in selecting candidates or getting a job—people who have always presumed that an interview was just a simple occasion for two people getting together to discuss what they are looking for and what they can offer, but who nevertheless instinctively feel there must be a correct method for going about it.

By and large the techniques adopted by the professionals, although frequently wrapped up in a lot of jargon, *are* simply a matter of common sense. This book is an uncomplicated resumé of them. After following the straightforward advice that it gives, those going for interview will know what is really required of them and how to present themselves to the best possible advantage; and inexperienced interviewers will be able to make better-informed comparisons and choices between candidates. The guidelines given may occasionally seem rather rigid but their purpose is to provide a readily comprehended procedure which can be adapted to suit the individual and situation concerned. Some people may like to follow them to the letter. Others may prefer to use them as a general plan and a stimulus for rethinking their whole attitude to the interview procedure and what it is supposed to discover.

For the majority of us the interview we are most likely to face is the job selection interview, and the first part of the book is structured round this. It deals with the applicant's experience first, looking at such topics as pre-interview preparation, questions to expect, questions to ask, appearance, and coping with the nervous-

1

ness which often leads to a poor interview performance from someone who would be confident and self-assured once they were actually doing the job. Because we have found that under stress it is easier to keep a grip on a few vital facts rather than generalities we have included several basic checklists.

Although on first consideration the interviewer might seem to have an easier task, interviewing constructively is a great skill. The pressure is on the interviewer to give the candidates the opportunity to reveal themselves in the best and most accurate light. Again, this book is not for those highly trained personnel staff who conduct interviews on behalf of others and who recruit into large companies. It is aimed at those who find themselves as interviewers as a result of what they do; people taking on extra help as a small business expands, for example; people who find themselves in management positions without any formal training; or parents looking to find reliable help to care for their children while they are at work. Almost inevitably making a mistake in the person you take on will be expensive, time-consuming and rather stressful as you try to extricate yourself, so it is only sensible to make yourself as skilled as possible in conducting an interview.

For interviewers and candidates alike one of the key themes running through the books is *methodical preparation*. It is as much what you do prior to the interview as during it that determines your performance. By reading this book and following the very simple guidelines we suggest you will quickly cross the dividing line between those who approach each interview in a haphazard fashion, not knowing what makes the difference between success and failure, and those who know what they want to get out of the interview situation and how they should go about it. To be really well prepared we suggest you read through the entire section from both points of view as it will give a good insight into what is going on in the other side's mind.

Although the majority of the book is taken up with employment interviewing there are also sections on getting the information you really want out of 'interviews' with professionals such as doctors; with being on both sides of the microphone in TV and radio interviews (relevant to many more people than ever before with the growth of local broadcasting) and interviews for university places.

By reading the book and realizing that an interview, from either side of the desk, is something that has its own rules and a technique that can be learned, you are already halfway to making sure you will

2

get what you want from the situation.

A general book of this nature is aimed at a wide range of people, from young people going for their first job to redundant executives. We have therefore covered an equally wide range when giving examples of suitable qualifications/answers, etc. These are simply examples; the underlying principles are the same, whatever the level at which you yourself are aiming.

For those who want to build on the fundamental skills to be learned from this book there is a comprehensive book list at the end, and a list of organizations which offer specialist training for several different categories of both interviewees *and* interviewers.

In conclusion we should like to thank all those many professionals who were so generous in their advice while we were compiling our material.

PART I

Employment Interviews—
The Candidate

Introduction:
What Makes a Successful
Candidate?

There is no magic formula which will always ensure the successful outcome of a job interview. There are too many variables, not least the calibre and suitability of the other people going for interview. Nonetheless it is possible to take steps to ensure that you are one of those who definitely has a chance of succeeding. The interview itself is really the final stage in a process which for the interviewee (and the interviewer!) should have started well before the moment when you go through the door of the interview room.

That process should culminate in your being an interview candidate with a thorough knowledge of your 'selling' points, having applied for a job for which you are genuinely suited, ready to counter any weak points in your skills/work history as positively as possible, able to present yourself in a confident and self-possessed manner.

Preparation—the key to a good interview

When you look through this book you may be surprised to see how much is dealt with apart from the actual form which the interview will follow. This is because it is the preparation you do beforehand, together with your own attitude to yourself and your work which will largely affect your performance at the interview itself. Much of what follows is only common sense. There are no complicated theories and tricks to master. Indeed it is all deceptively simple. Yet most people who go for interviews that may have an important effect on the next few years of their lives still do so inadequately prepared to show themselves in the best possible light. Being good at interviews is a skill quite separate from your work skills and it is one which is not difficult to master. There are two fundamental rules, *'Be prepared!'* and *'Be positive about yourself.'*

1

Before the Interview

Applying for the right jobs

Whether you are out of work and applying for a lot of jobs, or in employment but looking to change, there is only any point in applying for positions where you have a real chance of being successful. To do this you must know: what you are capable of, what you want out of a job, and your weak spots so that you are prepared to counter any negative questioning. It is bad for morale, and therefore bad for your performance in subsequent interviews, if you are constantly rejected because you are clearly unsuitable for the jobs for which you apply.

There are therefore two important pieces of preparation which you should make before you even apply for a job, let alone go for an interview for it.

Self-assessment

First sit down and make a list of your plus and minus points. A thorough self-assessment will help you get totally clear in your own mind what you are most suited for and what you actually want. This will make you a far more positive candidate in any interview. It will also give you a more objective idea of how an employer sees you when reading your application form or letter. You can then begin to emphasize your strong points and do something to counteract negative ones.

Method

The easiest and most obvious way to go about this self-assessment is to divide a sheet of paper with a line down the middle, head it 'Plus' and 'Minus' and write down everything you can think of under each heading. Some points may be linked to both sides of the paper. For example, you may be someone who does not enjoy the enforced camaraderie of office life. On the other hand, the plus side of that may be that you are good at working alone without constant supervision. If you find self-assessment a difficult exercise, and you probably will, then you might like to consult people whose opinion you respect and whom you feel really know you, maybe former colleagues or former teachers. Try to remember anything for which others have praised or criticized you. Don't be too embarrassed or shy actually to write down what you think is *good* about yourself. It is important to be honest with yourself so that you can learn to match yourself reasonably accurately with jobs for which you are genuinely suited.

Include out-of-work activities

Remember that for young people just beginning work and women returning to paid employment, activities outside work can be a useful indicator of potential and may even contribute to greater working skills.

You may surprise yourself by how good your qualifications are when you look at them closely. Most of us have a tendency to underrate our own skills and experience, especially if we cannot put a definite name to them. If you are a dentist or a forklift truck driver it is easy to tell others what your skills are. If you are a shop assistant who frequently deputizes for the manager of a busy store you may need some prompting to realize that among your qualifications you 'are ready to take responsibility', 'have a flexible approach to work', and 'are used to dealing with the public'.

For example, if you were able to work out a new method of organizing stock shelves so that components were more quickly available to people on the factory floor this would show perfectly that you 'are able to show initiative'. If you were promoted from general secretarial duties to organizing the flow of work through the typing pool you can assume you 'have qualities of leadership and organizational skills'.

There are also many less 'aggressive' qualities which you may possess. If you do not feel you are a thrusting, dynamic sort of person you may possess different but equally desirable qualities which employers will want. You may be honest, reliable, trust-worthy, caring and good at handling people, to name a few examples.

Some questions which may be useful in self-assessment

- What are my educational achievements?
- Which were my best subjects at school?

- What extracurricular activities was I involved with at school?
- What does this show about my interests?
- What does this show about my ability to show initiative and organizational skills?
- What training have I had since leaving school?
- What jobs have I had since leaving full-time education?
- What extra skills have I learned through doing those jobs?
- Why am I looking for a new job?
- Do I prefer working on my own or as part of a team?
- What does that tell me about myself?
- What sort of jobs do I find myself attracted to?
- What do I want out of my working life?
- How successful have I been at various jobs?
- How did the company benefit from having me on the staff?
- Which work have I found most satisfying?
- Which work have I found easiest?
- Which work have I most disliked?
- Which work have I found most difficult?
- What have I been praised for at work?
- What have I been criticized for at work?
- What has my reaction been to criticism?
- What has my reaction been to praise?
- Is job security important to me?
- How would I describe myself?
- How do I think others would describe me?
- What books/newspapers do I read?
- What television programmes do I watch?
- What extra efforts have I made to increase my general skills (night school, etc.)?
- What do I do in my spare time?
- What would my attitude be if asked to move in order to take a job?
- What would my attitude be if I had a difficult or long journey to work?
- Would I be prepared to take less money in order to retrain for something new?
- Would I be prepared to take less money for doing a 'caring' job or one which is very creative?
- Do I have any family commitments which restrict the sort of job I can take on?
- Can I drive, type, operate a VDU, etc?

11

- Am I stimulated or frightened by the thought of change?
- What is my age?
- How might that be seen as a problem?
- How can I show it is an advantage?
- How have I demonstrated that I have initiative/staying power/ leadership qualities/flexibility/get on well with people/can work without supervision?

NB Add to this list any qualities which repeatedly appear in descriptions of the type of work you are interested in.

If there is someone you trust and who knows you well you could ask for their opinions on some of these questions and your answers to them.

Remember your 'plus' points during the interview

Time spent collecting concrete evidence that you possess these and similar skills and qualities which are often expressed in rather general terms will pay off handsomely when you are required to prove your worth in an interview. Young people, the unemployed and women returning to work after a long period at home will have to show extra ingenuity to extract evidence of their work skills and potential from their life history.

'Plus' points for school-leavers

Young people should emphasize extra projects, responsibilities and activities at school or college. Evidence can be found in extra-curricular activities as well. Being involved in running the students' union shows many possible qualities—initiative, ability to communicate, organizational skills, energy and responsibility to name a few. Part-time work to help pay for studies shows a positive attitude, resourcefulness, hard work, discipline and valuable experience of the working world.

'Plus' points for the unemployed

Similarly, unemployed people who can show they have used their time constructively, in study or voluntary work for example, will be able to match themselves to jobs demanding the qualities this demonstrates—initiative, hard work, flexibility, reliability, etc.— and possibly pick up some useful skills and experience at the same time. Being aware yourself that your potential has not been allowed to waste away will increase the confidence of your performance in the interview. Of course you should also list experience and skill gained from past employment.

'Plus' points for women returning to work

Unfortunately not enough value is placed in the working world on the organizational and management skills acquired in running a home and family efficiently. Former full-time housewives should search around for evidence of skills other than domestic ones. Driving is a useful skill, starting or running a parent–teacher association is proof of many useful abilities and qualities, fund-raising for charity demonstrates energy, initiative and organizational ability. These examples will not immediately take you to being chairperson of ICI but they will give you personally, as well as potential employers, a more positive image of you as a candidate in an interview.

Positive interpretation of weaknesses

Be honest about assessing your weak points as well. Nobody has perfect qualifications and a perfect work record. Everyone has had some disappointment or failure. The important thing is to be aware of these weak points yourself so that you can be prepared with the best positive interpretation of them if the interviewer picks them up. For example, if you were sacked you can be prepared, *not* with a feeble-sounding excuse, 'The office manager and I didn't hit it off, he was a very difficult man', but with a positive statement, 'Yes, the job didn't suit me and I was asked to leave but I was lucky enough to get a place on a word-processing course so I was much better prepared for my next job and I stayed for two years'.

If you have a friend or colleague with whom you can practise it is a good idea to get used to hearing yourself say these positive statements out loud. We are all far too inclined to apologize for ourselves.

A typical self-assessment sheet might look like this:

Plus	Minus
1 Good education up to x standard	1 Not good at figures (failed maths examination)
2 Experience of living and working abroad; good knowledge of French	2 Easily annoyed by sloppy standards in others

3 Get on well with people	3 Present firm slow to adopt new technology, less experience in most up-to-date equipment
4 Training and experience as a VDU operator	4 Several changes of job in 18-month period 197x–7x
5 Prepared to be flexible, not requiring a set routine	5 Six-month period out of work 198x–8x
6 Management experience running own department	6 Not keen to move at the moment while children at school
7 Interested in home computers, doing some programming	7 Too inclined to compare self unfavourably with others
8 Involved in community work, use organizational skills outside work	
9 Good driver, clean licence	

Using self-assessment for your curriculum vitae (c.v.)

This self-assessment list will also be useful when you compile your most important self-selling document—your curriculum vitae (c.v.) (see p. 24). A short summary of what you regard as your strong points makes an excellent final paragraph to distinguish you from other candidates.

Matching yourself to the job

When you have made an initial assessment of your strengths and weaknesses you will find it easier to recognize work for which you are genuinely suited.

You can then apply a similar method to the second major piece of preparation before applying for a job: matching yourself to the job for which you might apply. Quite simply this means *working out what is needed and seeing how you can supply it*. This will:

(a) make it easier to ensure that your application form/letter underlines what suits you to the job. You will then have a better chance of getting through to the interview stage;

(b) make you aware of what you should emphasize to the

interviewer to demonstrate your suitability for the post;
(c) forewarn you of some of the less favourable aspects that the interviewer might pick up on. You will therefore be prepared with good answers when confronted with searching questions.

Method

Again the simplest way to gain a clear picture is to divide a sheet of paper into two columns and ask yourself some obvious questions.

On the left-hand side list the skills and qualifications required in the job description, or what you yourself know from experience the job will entail.

On the right-hand side try to match your own qualifications, strengths and experience to the requirements. If you have already taken the trouble to make a searching assessment of yourself as a candidate this should not be impossibly difficult.

Some questions to see how you match up to the job

- What does this job involve?
- What will be expected of me?
- Have I done anything like it before?
- What qualifications are they looking for?
- Do I have those qualifications?
- Do I have any other qualifications which might be an advantage?
- What experience are they looking for?
- Do I have that experience?
- Do I have any other experience which might be helpful?
- What skills are they looking for?
- Do I have those skills?
- If not, could I learn them?
- What qualities do they want?
- Do I have those qualities?
- How can I prove I have those qualities?
- Do I have any additional qualities which would make me suitable?
- How much responsibility would I have?
- Does the advertisement specify a certain age range?
- Am I the right age?
- If not, can I present my age as an advantage?
- What is the salary?

- Is this within the salary range I think I need?
- Where is the job located?
- Would I be able to arrive there on time?
- Would the fares take up too much of the money?
- Would I have to move and would I be prepared to?
- Why am I applying for this particular job?
- What can I contribute to the job?
- Will the job fit in with my family commitments?
- Why do I think I can do the job better than the other applicants?
- Is there anyone who would act as a referee or recommend me for the job?

A job match sheet might look like this:

Book-keeper

Small antiques firm in Norwich seeks mature, hard-working person, experienced, PAYE and VAT. Applicant must have pleasant outgoing personality and flexible approach to work.

Age 30–45   Hours 8.00 a.m.–4.00 p.m.
Salary £X,000 p.a.

Job requirements	My qualifications
Age	Within age range
Experienced book-keeper PAYE/VAT	Qualified to take books trial balance. Experience of PAYE and VAT as book-keeper to small electronics firm and solicitor's office.
Antiques firm	Experience of helping and doing book-keeping in parents' kitchen-ware shop. Interested in collecting antiques.
Norwich	Live 5 miles (8 km) outside, own car so no problems getting in to work by 8.00 a.m.
Mature/hard working	Stable private life. Good references and good work record including work at weekends and vacations while studying.

Pleasant personality	Former employers will vouch for ability to fit in with small staff.
Flexible approach	Helped as sales representative at trade exhibitions when working for electronics firm. Would welcome chance to learn more about antiques trade and help in shop. Ready to be flexible over working hours.

Possible liabilities

Presently unemployed (6 months) because of takeover of small electronics firm by larger company.

Positive response

The *job* was made redundant not me as a person. Have used spare time to begin business administration course (postal tuition), also furniture restoring at local college. Kept skills sharp by doing book-keeping for parents' shop.

Applying for a job

Obviously you will only be asked to come for an interview if you have made an initial approach for a job. This application itself can get you off to a good or bad start. It may predispose the interviewer to accept you if nothing untoward is revealed at the interview, or it may prevent you from ever reaching that stage.

Putting out 'feelers'

It is important to remember that a very large percentage of jobs never come on to the open market but are filled from within the firm, by people applying 'on spec.' or by people who hear about a vacancy from friends or colleagues working in the same field. If you are unemployed or actively looking to change your job you will increase your chances immeasurably if you let other people know and make a positive effort to follow up any leads you receive.

Job exhibitions

An increasingly common way for companies to find new recruits is by taking a stand at a job exhibition, often based on one particular industry or trade. Personnel staff are able to conduct 'instant' interviews and applicants are able to make immediate contact with a large number of employers. The same guidelines apply as at more conventional interviews, including presenting yourself confidently and being smartly dressed. It is a good idea to take along a number of copies of your c.v. which you can leave with prospective employers. On these occasions you may be offered a job on the spot, so it is very important to have a good understanding of what you want and need from a job before you go. Be confident and try to approach as many stands as you can. At the very least job exhibitions give you a good chance to practise your interviewing technique.

Applying by telephone

At its simplest a job application can be a telephone call in response to an advertisement or because you hear there may be a vacancy with a company. Even at this level preparation pays off, so:

(a) have enough money with you if you are calling from a public telephone so that you are not constantly interrupted by the pip-pip-pip sound or cut off because you run out of change;

(b) know the name of the person you should speak to (if it appears in the advertisement) or ask to speak to the personnel department. If you speak to someone in the department ask if you can have their name in case you need to telephone again;

(c) have a checklist ready by the telephone for any information you will need before definitely applying for the job. For instance, you may want to know about training, holidays or canteen facilities (see p. 27 on gathering background information);

(d) have a pencil and paper ready to take down interview details—dates, times, names and travel information, if you are able to make arrangements over the telephone;

(e) check that you have taken the details correctly before you hang up.

It will probably not go unnoticed if you appear well organized at this stage, and it will certainly help you to appear at the right place and at the right time looking calm and unruffled.

Applying by letter

For many jobs a letter is the usual way of applying. This allows you to make a more considered approach than a telephone call and to use the job matching list you have drawn up to bring to the employer's attention the reasons why you are suitable for the job and why you should be seen for interview.

By and large it is better to write an individually tailored application letter for each job, as this gives the company the feeling that you have a particular interest in that specific job. However, those who are unemployed, especially if they have been for some time, may find it is more important to send out as many letters as possible, in the hope of getting some response. They might prefer to work out a general letter and simply insert the details such as where they saw the job advertised and the name given to the vacancy advertised.

Whether writing in response to an advertisement or making a general enquiry about work, the following points apply

(a) Write in your own handwriting, unless it is so bad it would be a point against you or you are a typist and a typewritten letter has been specified. Potential employers feel they can tell a lot about a person by their handwriting.

(b) Spell correctly any names or titles used in an advertisement or you will give the impression that you are careless and slipshod (if you are a weak speller get someone to check the letter over for you).

(c) Refer to where you saw the vacancy advertised.

(d) Give brief details of yourself and any relevant experience or qualifications to show why you are interested in the particular job or are a suitable candidate for a general interview.

(e) Enclose your c.v. (see p. 26) and mention this in the letter.

(f) Finish on a positive note with a phrase like 'I look forward to hearing from you'.

(g) Sign 'Yours sincerely' if you are sending the letter to a named individual. 'Yours faithfully' if the letter begins 'Dear Sir' or 'Dear Madam'.

NB If an advertisement says, 'write for application form' then keep the letter very brief and *without* personal details as you will only have to repeat them on the form later.

A typical letter of application may appear as in Fig. 1 on p. 21.

Advertisement

Experienced stock controller

Ref. BE/130/S

Frozen food factory requires stock controller to run main warehouse. Applicant should be familiar with all standard procedures for control of food storage. Experience of large-scale warehouse preferred.

Salary commensurate with age and experience.

Write to: R. Smith
Personnel Officer
Hendry's Frozen Foods
Ladysmith Road
Birmingham B19 3SJ

Figures 1 and 2 show sample letters.

In some cases the response to your letter or telephone call will be a definite appointment to come for an interview. If you have written in response to an advertisement they may ask you to telephone to arrange a suitable time for the interview. If so make sure your telephone call is an organized one (see p. 18 above).

Application forms

Sometimes you will be required to fill in an application form which will be used to select candidates for interview. Like your letter of application the application form will give the interviewer a picture of you before you actually arrive for the interview. It will therefore affect what happens during the interview, and if it is not done well enough it may prevent you reaching the interview stage at all. So it is vitally important to complete the form to show yourself in the best possible light.

Keeping your own copy

Because points arising from the application form may be discussed during the interview, it is a good idea to keep a copy for yourself if the application form is a complicated one. You can then check through before the interview to ensure that you are consistent in what you say about yourself. Although any discrepancies may seem trivial, interviewers will regard everything you say with suspicion if

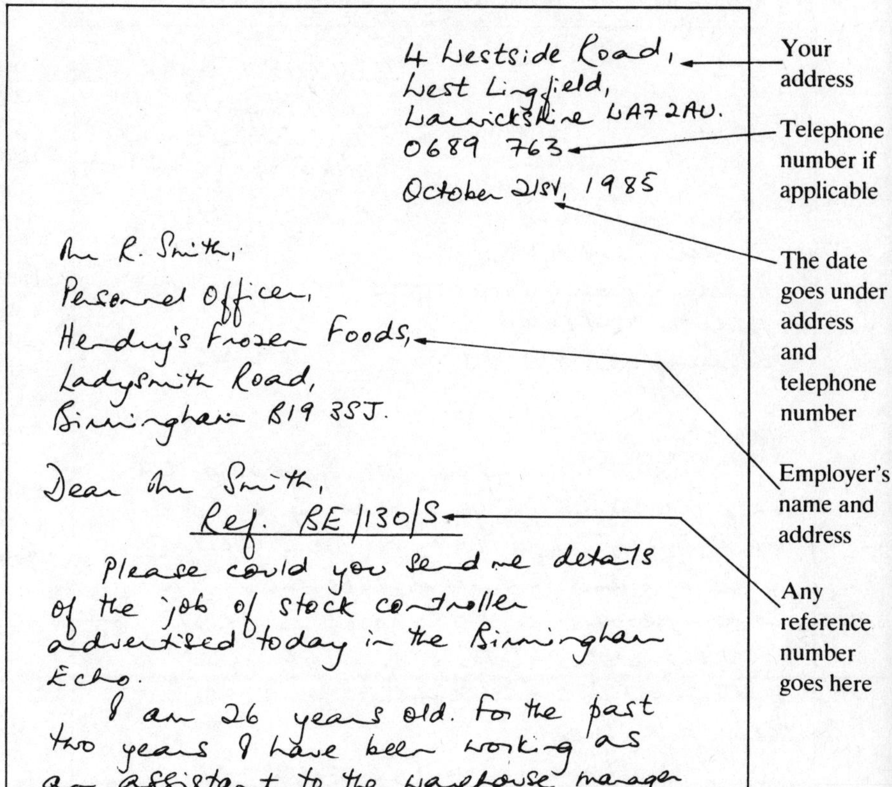

4 Westside Road,
West Lingfield,
Warwickshire WA7 2AU.
0689 763
October 21st, 1985

Mr R. Smith,
Personnel Officer,
Hendry's Frozen Foods,
Ladysmith Road,
Birmingham B19 3SJ.

Dear Mr Smith,

    Ref. BE/130/S

    Please could you send me details of the job of stock controller advertised today in the Birmingham Echo.

    I am 26 years old. For the past two years I have been working as an assistant to the warehouse manager at Troughton's meat processing plant in Coventry, where my work has been mainly concerned with stock control.

    I enclose further details of my qualifications and experience on a separate sheet.

    I look forward to hearing from you

    Yours sincerely,
    Michael Johnson.

Annotations (right margin):

- Your address
- Telephone number if applicable
- The date goes under address and telephone number
- Employer's name and address
- Any reference number goes here

Figure 1

If you have written a speculative letter it might look like this:

4 Westside Road —
West Linfield
Warwickshire WA72AV
0689-763
October 21st 1985

The Personnel Officer,
Hendy's Frozen Foods,
Ladysmith Road,
Birmingham B19 3SJ.

Dear Sir,

I am writing to ask if you have any vacancies in your packing or warehousing departments. I am twenty-six years old and have had experience as a warehouseman and in stock control.

I enclose details of my qualifications and experience on a separate sheet.

I do hope you will consider me for any vacancies which arise and I look forward to hearing from you.

Yours faithfully,

Michael Johnson.

Labels on the right margin:

Your address

Telephone number applicant

The date goes under address and telephone number

Employer name and address

Figure 2

22

they find that you have apparently lied on one particular answer. This applies at every level of employment.

If you receive an application form as a response to a job application or as a preliminary to an interview it should be filled in and returned promptly. If you allow more than one or two days to elapse you may either lose your nerve, or find that you have missed your opportunity, or you might give the prospective employer the impression that you are not really interested. It is best to return the form by first-class post.

Filling in the form

Before you begin to fill in any application form make sure you have read and thoroughly understood any accompanying notes.

Unless your handwriting is illegible, or the form specifically asks for typewriting, the form should be neatly handwritten. Black ink is best as the interviewer may want to take photocopies.

Never begin filling in the real form until you have practised at least once on a photocopy.

Check spelling and grammar on the copy before filling in the real form. Ask someone to check these for you if you are uncertain.

Where there are answers requiring some thought draft them first. Copy the final version on to the form only when you are fully satisfied with what you have written.

Be brief and to the point. Employers may be sifting through dozens of forms and unwilling to plough through a lot of waffle.

If there is a space headed 'spare-time activities' or 'other information', use it to show yourself in a positive light. Use your self-assessment sheet as a reminder and fill in the sort of activities which will show that you are an enthusiastic hard-working person. If you are a keen gardener or have done any fund-raising or interesting travelling, for example, you will appear a more attract-ive candidate than someone who simply spends their spare time slumped in front of the television.

Filling in forms at the interview

If possible avoid filling in forms at the time of the interview as you will not do your best while nervous, nor will you be able to correct mistakes easily or make changes. Ask if you can take the form away with you and put it in the post the same day, or bring it back later. If that is allowed you must get it back to the interviewer as soon as possible. If it is not allowed then try and fill it in immediately afterwards when the pressure is off. If you have already given thought to your self-assessment and how well your qualifications match the job you will make a better showing on the form than if you have not bothered. Whatever happens, *do not be pressured into filling in a form quickly*.

Preparing a c.v. (career history)

A curriculum vitae or c.v., sometimes called a career history, is a valuable tool in helping your job application reach the interview stage.

The main aim of the c.v. is to give a prospective employer a brief resumé of your education, qualifications, training, experience, strengths and successes so that you will be given the chance of an interview. Send it whenever you are applying for a job 'on spec.' or where no mention is made in an advertisement of an application form (which usually covers the same type of information).

A c.v. should be short (no more than one side of a sheet of paper), concise, and give a positive picture of you and your achievements. Every c.v. will be different because every work record and experience is different.

The c.v. of a school leaver will be almost entirely about educational achievements and any pastimes, experiences or interests which indicate the type of person an employer will be looking for. An older person will also list employment experience, with the emphasis on achievement. A prospective employer's interest will be focused on the last ten years approximately, so experiences before that can be telescoped into a short sentence or two. However, you must give a continuous thread back to schooldays, otherwise an unexplained gap may provoke awkward questions and negative thinking in the person reading the career history.

Never 'bad mouth' any company or person for whom you have worked. This creates a very negative impression in what should be a totally positive document.

Presenting the information

There are two schools of thought about whether or not the information should be presented chronologically (which gives a picture of the person's career development) or in the reverse order, where the emphasis is on current work and achievement. You must decide which approach suits you best. However, if the employer has specifically asked for a chronological c.v. then make sure it is presented the way it is requested, even if it means rethinking the standard version you usually send out. Failure to do so will give the impression that you have not taken much trouble with your application and may be careless in the future.

Referees

You may like to add the name of one or two referees to your c.v., either to vouch for your general honesty and reliability or to confirm that you have the skills and experience you claim in the c.v. It is most important that you get permission from the people you name before you start sending your c.v. forms out to prospective employers.

When compiling the c.v. leave a small space at the top of the form to enter the job name and reference number, if any, of the job for which you are applying.

Ideally the c.v. should be typed, not handwritten. Use the best quality paper, and if you are getting several photocopies made make sure they are done on good quality paper and not ordinary photocopy paper.

Although it is a good idea to make several copies at a time of your c.v., especially if you are going to apply for a lot of jobs 'on spec.', do not get too many done at once. You may well want to change things, adding new or different information, when you have had a little more experience of what people are looking for.

Ready-printed c.v./application forms

It is now possible to buy excellent ready-printed job application forms. These are in effect c.v. forms which you complete with your own personal and career details. They come with stubs that you fill in with the date and details of your application, brief notes and the result, to form a mini-interview file. They can be used simply as c.v. forms and are particularly useful when you are applying for jobs 'on spec.' as you can get all the relevant information on one neat form which looks efficient and will not overwhelm the recipient. They require a brief accompanying letter. Details of where they can be obtained are given on p. 146.

Space →
to
enter
details
of
job
applied
for

Personal information
Name: Joan Anderson

Address: 11 The Close, Evesham, Worcs.

Telephone: (home) Evesham 7612   (day) Evesham 3987
Date of birth: June 1962   Marital status: Married

Education and training
1974–80   Tanglewood Comprehensive, Evesham, 5 O-
Levels: English Language, English Literature,
French, Domestic Science, Mathematics
1 A-Level: English (grade D)
1980–81   Secretarial studies, Birmingham Technical College
(Distinction in office practice and typing)

Employment history
Nov. 1981–   Russell Engineering Services, Birmingham
June 1983   General secretarial, then personal secretary to
Mr John Brown, Sales Executive
I had experience of many different departments
including Research and Development and
Personnel, where I helped to put the files on
computer.
Sept. 1983–   Blake, Thwaites & Blake, Solicitors, Chestnut
Road, Evesham
Personal secretary to Mr Anthony Blake
Notice required from present job—1 month

Referees
Mrs Kathleen Turner, Lecturer, Birmingham Technical
College
Mr John Brown, Russell Engineering Services, Birmingham

Other interests
Keeping and showing Siamese cats; restoring old sports cars.
I also enjoy the cinema and walking.

Additional information
I left Russell Engineering Services when I married and
moved back to Evesham. I have had a good deal of
experience on a word processor and am very ready to adapt
to new office techniques and equipment.

Figure 3

26

Professionally written c.v.s

If you think you would like professional help to draw up your c.v., there are several firms that specialize in doing this, and they generally advertise in the personal columns of the upmarket daily newspapers. A typical c.v. format might look like Figure 3.

Gathering background information about the job and about the company

Eventually some of your replies to advertisements or general enquiries about vacancies will result in your being called for an interview. As soon as you have a date fixed, or even before you hear, it is a good idea to start gathering background information about the job for which you have applied and the people for whom you would be working. It may even be that despite taking care with matching yourself to the job before making an initial application you may find out further information that will make you less enthusiastic about the job. More importantly, the better informed you are the better your interview performance will be.

Find out about salary/holidays/conditions before *the interview*

Interviewees sometimes think that when an interviewer says to them, 'Do you have any questions you would like to ask me?' this is an opportunity to ask how long the holidays are and how soon you would be due for a pay rise. Unfortunately such questions may give a negative impression of your priorities. The interviewer would rather hear you ask positive questions about the company, about training opportunities and the chance to progress to greater responsibility.

It is almost always possible to find out the answers to basic questions about pay and conditions prior to the interview. This way you will have a better idea of whether the job will suit you, you avoid wasting your and the interviewer's time, and you sidestep one possibility of creating a negative impression.

If you do not automatically receive literature covering basic information when you are called for an interview, telephone or write and ask if there is any available. If no printed matter exists you should ask to speak to the person mentioned in the interview letter, or the personnel department, the training officer or the training manager and get the answers to the most important questions.

If possible go to collect this information in person (telephone beforehand if that makes you more confident), unless the company is very small and you would feel conspicuous. An advance visit gives you a chance to assess what the firm is like, what the other people are like and also how they dress, so that you can go appropriately dressed for the interview. You may also get a chance to ask someone a little about the firm and about working conditions. A visit before the interview can also act as a dummy run to help you get there in good time on the day itself.

Checklist of questions for your own information to be answered before the interview

- Where will I be working?
- What is the salary?
- When is the salary reviewed?
- Is there a pension plan?
- Is the pension plan contributory or non-contributory?
- Is there an annual bonus?
- How will I be paid?
- What are the holidays?
- Will my present holiday arrangements be honoured?
- What is transport like?
- Is it possible to park?
- Are there canteen facilities?
- Are there luncheon vouchers?
- Is there any overtime?
- Is there extra pay for overtime?
- Is there any weekend working?
- Is there any late working?
- Is there a high staff turnover?
- Is the company well enough established to offer job security?
- Why does the vacancy exist?
- May I meet the person who is leaving?
- Who will I be working for?
- Are there organized training facilities and opportunities?
- Is there a company nurse?
- What is the attitude to leave for taking care of sick children?
- What are the opportunities for promotion?
- When would I be expected to start?

Keep this information in your *interview file* (see p. 30).

Thorough background information on the company will improve your interview performance

Not only will you want to know about basics like salaries and pensions, but you will also want to find out as much as possible about the firm and its product and methods. This will enable you to show the interviewer that you are really keen for a job with that particular company. Many potential employers complain that applicants come to them with a poor knowledge of what the job involves and no particular interest in the company. It is only common sense that an interviewer will be interested in a candidate who actually shows some enthusiasm for the job and the firm.

People who are applying for executive and management positions should most definitely do everything they can to make themselves fully conversant with the company, its product and its trading position. It is perfectly in order to ask for a copy of the *annual report*, the *balance sheet* and any other *promotional material* as soon as you have been called for interview, or even beforehand. Public reference libraries keep information on the larger companies. It also makes sense to ask around among other people in the same field to see if you can pick up any extra information about the firm.

Checklist of questions to ask about the company so that you are well informed before the interview

- What does the firm make/sell?
- How big is the company?
- Where is it located?
- How is it organized?
- What is its turnover?
- What is its profitability?
- Who are its customers?
- What are the career prospects with the company?
- How secure would a job be with this company?
- What kind of workers do they already have?
- How many workers are there?
- What do I know about their recent performance/trading history?
- Is the work environment pleasant?

Background information about the interviewer is helpful

You will be at an advantage if you know a little about the person who will interview you before you arrive. This is especially important when the job is quite high powered and the interview may be rather searching. Try to find out at the very least what position the interviewer holds with the company and whether you will be working directly with him or her. Even better, ask around and find out what sort of person the interviewer is, his/her likes and dislikes. 'Forewarned is forearmed' is an appropriate cliché in this situation.

Keep all background information in your interview file (see below) together with any printed information obtained from the company.

Keeping interview files

The aim of all the preparation and information gathering prior to the interview is to ensure:

(a) that you get called for interview;
(b) that you arrive at the interview as well informed as possible and therefore in the most confident and self-assured state of mind.

It is essential if you are to have a clear mind about each particular job and interview that you keep your applications and all the information relevant to them methodically filed and easily accessible.

Keep the paperwork and notes for each application in a separate folder or large envelope. These can be reused as necessary.

If your application was in response to a particular advertisement keep the advertisement stapled to the front of the folder.

If you applied 'on spec.' write the name, address and telephone number of the company on the front, together with the name of any contact you have there.

In the file you should keep:

(a) all the background literature and information you receive from the company. Read it first and keep it in this file ready to refresh your memory at the last moment;
(b) notes of all the answers you have received to questions about pay and conditions of work;
(c) notes you have made to fill you in on the background and performance of the company:
(d) your own copies of your application form and/or letter of application:

A typical interview plan might look like this:

JOB

Company name and address
Contact

Date advertised/applied for:
Person to see for interview:
Date/time of interview:

How to get there:
How long will it take to travel/park:

Background information

Remember to ask about:

Expect to hear by:

Date to make follow-up call:

Points learned from the interview:

Figure 4

(e) if you receive an interview appointment, file a reminder of whom you are seeing, the time of your appointment and how to get there.

(f) follow-up notes including a note of a date to telephone if you have not received any news from the interview and what you have learned from the interview (see p. 63 follow-up for interviewees).

Making an interview plan

A lot of this information can be kept together on one sheet of paper to make an interview plan (Figure 4).

Keep a diary

If you do not have one already get yourself a diary which is small enough to carry with you. Note down all your appointments and any follow-up dates when you expect to hear results or ought to telephone for information. You can also use it to make brief notes/ reminders and for keeping essential telephone numbers. A diary is an essential tool if you are aiming to improve your overall efficiency.

2

Going for the Interview

You have an interview appointment. You know you are not wasting your time because this is a job for which you are genuinely suited and which you would like. Your immediate concern is how to make yourself the candidate most likely to succeed!

Punctuality

The first step towards success is, rather obviously, to get to your appointment in good time. That means reporting to the receptionist about 15 minutes before the time of your interview. Punctuality always gives a good impression and if you cut things fine you will not be as calm and confident as you should be. If you are late you may irritate the interviewer or lose your appointment altogether.

Make sure that you have the correct address for the interview, which may not always be the same as the company's main address.

Next, find out the best means of getting there. Make sure of the times of trains, the numbers of the buses, the line of the underground, the route if you are driving. If parking is difficult in a built-up area it may be better to go by public transport.

Finally, work out how long the journey will take you, including finding the right office. Do not forget to take the rush hour into account. Leave yourself enough time to get from the station or bus stop or to park your car without hurrying. Do a dummy run if necessary, you will then be sure you are setting out in good time.

If you are late

If, in spite of all your forward planning, you find you are going to be late, try to telephone the office so that the interview can be rescheduled. Being late will count against you far less if no one has been kept waiting around as a result.

If you are late, apologize in a straightforward way with a brief reason. A long, involved excuse always sounds less convincing.

Being polite to everyone you meet

Whether you are late or early it is wise and makes for a far pleasanter experience to be polite and pleasant to everyone you come in contact with, both before and after the interview. This includes people like tea ladies and receptionists. The nicer you are to them the more they will help to put you at your ease. What is more, you can never be sure who will be asked for their opinion of you after you have left, especially if it is a question of whether or not you will fit in well with the rest of the staff.

Appearance

Research shows that people form 90 per cent of their opinion of you within a minute and a half of meeting you. In an interview you are not going to have time to correct them if they are wrong. The impression you create is given as much by how you look and behave as by what you say and this very definitely includes what you wear.

Avoid extremes

It cannot be stressed too often that employers are very wary of extremes. This means that you should not turn up in casual clothes which express your out-of-work personality, enchanting as that may be, nor should you wear the sort of 'best' clothes which would make you the star at a party but which are patently unsuitable for day-to-day working situations. Being dressed completely in very dark colours gives a negative message. So, too, does wearing sunglasses as this is a positive gesture to prevent the interviewer from seeing your eyes and guessing what is going on in your mind.

Try and put yourself in the employer's place, or perhaps in the place of one of the people you may be dealing with as the employer's representative. What sort of person would you want to be met with if you had business to do with the company? What kind of person would you find reassuring? Your answer may give you a guide to the sort of clothes to wear for the interview. If you have the opportunity to visit the workplace in advance you can see the type of clothes which people are wearing and wear something similar. The more you look as though you will fit in the better.

Of course some jobs may actually require very casual clothes or special working clothes, in which case clearly you should not wear something similar for the interview. Instead choose something which is fairly formal, conservative and unstartling and which looks immaculately clean and tidy.

Men

For men the question of what to wear is nearly always answered by a suit. Naturally it should be clean and unrumpled and worn with a clean shirt and shoes. Hair should be fairly conservatively cut. The aim is to give an initial impression of efficiency; if you cannot even get your own act together what likelihood is there of your being of any use to anyone else? Taking trouble about your appearance is also a good sign that the job is important to you and is encouraging to a prospective employer.

Women

For women the question of what to wear is slightly more complex simply because there are more options. However, the same guidelines apply. Do not be tempted to go to extremes. Go for a fairly formal and conservative outfit, probably a suit, and keep hair under control. Some people still find trousers unacceptable female attire so play safe and stick to skirts unless you feel strongly on the subject. Do not wear excessive jewellery, especially if it is the sort which jangles. The cleaner and better groomed you look the greater will be the impression of efficiency and being in command of the situation which you give to the interviewer.

Try your clothes out before the interview

It is important that what you wear is comfortable. Practise wearing your interview outfit in advance. You do not want to find out in the interview itself that the skirt rides up disconcertingly high when you sit down or that the front gapes open when you lean forward to talk.

Avoid an interview 'uniform'

Some people suggest having one special, safe interview outfit. While it is a good idea to have something in which you feel confident and comfortable, and which is not getting 'tired', it may have disadvantages. If you go for a number of interviews without success you may subconsciously associate your interview outfit with failure. This does not necessarily mean paying out a lot of money for several totally new changes of clothes. Men can ring the changes by wearing a different shirt or tie if they don't want to invest in more than one suit. Women can wear different colour tights, or a new scarf or shirt. The aim is to avoid going into an interview feeling stale and with a 'here we go again' feeling.

If you are recalled for a second interview it is worth changing to a different outfit altogether if you can afford it or have something else suitable. If you wear the same thing twice in the same situation you may give the impression that you have one safe set of clothes and that you are only immaculately turned out when relying on that one safe outfit.

Avoid clutter

Do not come to an interview encumbered with a lot of clutter like parcels, scarves, large shopping bags, and shoulder bags, which make you look burdened down. If you need to bring an umbrella, a street guide or anything other than a briefcase or handbag leave it in the reception area during the interview.

Body language

Creating an overall impression

Giving time and thought to your appearance and the way in which you present yourself to others is not trivial. Your clothes are a means of communicating with other people. So too are your gestures, and the overall message they give is known as *body language*. It is vitally important because non-verbal signals tell other people as much about you as what you actually say to them. Many people—indeed many interviewers—are inclined to give more importance to how you behave than to what you say and management courses now include lessons on body language and how to interpret it.

The interviewer may be expecting certain answers and qualifications from the person she/he is interviewing but the overall impression of yourself which you create in the interview is equally important.

Giving a little thought to body language beforehand will get you off to a good start.

First impressions

The first impression the interviewer will have of you is as you come through the door. Knock on the door and as soon as you are invited to do so walk in confidently and *smiling*. Do not put your head tentatively round the door as if to check whether or not you are really wanted. Women in particular should be on guard against apologizing for themselves indirectly by this sort of tentative behaviour. For many reasons they often lack the superficial self-confidence of men, especially if they have been tied up by domesticity for years. Similarly very young people may have an unconfident approach. While it is wise to show a certain deference to those older than you who have been doing the job for years and who would be alienated by over-confident brashness, you must not look as though you might be a drag on whoever you are hoping to work with.

Basically interviewers are hoping that the answer to all their prayers is going to come walking through that door. Come in looking as though you might be able to solve an interviewer's problems, not as though you will bring a whole lot of problems of your own.

Posture

You will tell the interviewer a lot about yourself by the way you move your body. Try to walk into the room with good posture, though not like a guardsman on parade. Stooping shoulders and rounded back are placatory signals and imply a dangerous lack of confidence. Similarly when you are sitting down you should try and keep a fairly straight back. A woman should place her handbag on the floor next to her to avoid the possibility of sitting defensively crouched over it on her lap.

The handshake

Shake hands with the interviewer and sit down when invited to do so, not before. People feel they can tell a lot from a handshake and they are quite right. The handshake is a basic gesture of friend-liness.

You are aiming to create a sense of likeability and equality. If you are too domineering in your handshake (and this may be to overcompensate for nerves) you will antagonize the interviewer who will subconsciously feel threatened on his/her own territory. On the other hand, if you appear too submissive you stand in danger of being dismissed as a bit of a weed.

(a) Do not be the one to initiate the handshake but be quick to respond to the interviewer's gesture.
(b) Do not shake hands in a grasping manner with the palm inclining downwards as this also shows a desire to dominate.
(c) Do not hold on to the interviewer's hand for too long as this signals overfamiliarity.
(d) Do not shake hands in a limp manner or use just the tips of the fingers as this gives the impression you are a weak character.

(e) Shakes hands firmly but do not get involved in a 'trial of strength' handshake.

If you are unsure what sort of a handshaker you are, practise a few times with a friend. Shaking hands is an important part of a mock interview (see p. 61).

Gestures which antagonize

Since the interviewer is looking for a reliable, self-confident, honest individual who knows how to be friendly without being irritatingly overfamiliar it is sensible to know some of the basic body language that will work against you as well as what will cause a favourable reaction. It is impossible to remember and keep track of all your gestures but you should be careful to *avoid the following*:

(a) lolling back in your chair in an over-relaxed way, possibly with your hands behind your head. This is far too overconfident for the situation and will cause a very bad reaction.

(b) getting too close to the interviewer. This invades his/her territory and makes the interviewer feel threatened.

(c) putting your hands in your pockets. Depending on the way you do it this can look insolent, aggressive or defensive.

(d) crossing your arms tightly in front of you. This is a very defensive position and will prevent a relaxed atmosphere from being established.

(e) placing your hands or fingers over your mouth when you speak. This is the classic gesture used by those who are not being totally honest. Even if you are resorting to it out of nervousness or fear that you have bad breath it will create a very negative impression on the interviewer.

(f) evading eye contact with the interviewer. This will make you look shifty even if it is only a result of nerves. On the other hand do not overcompensate and regard the interviewer with a fixed stare.

Irritating mannerisms

Some mannerisms may not be of great use to the interviewer in assessing your character but they may work against you by being irritating. Always remember that most people form a basic opinion about you within two minutes of meeting you. Think of some of the actions which have led you to form instant opinions about others, either favourable or unfavourable, and you will realize how quickly and easily it happens. 'He talks a lot, he must be conceited.' 'She never looks up, she must have something to hide.'

Interviews make people nervous and unfortunately many of our most irritating mannerisms are those into which we retreat when under pressure. Talking too much and avoiding people's eyes are just two of them. Others are mumbling, excessive fidgeting, slumping into the chair, giving one-syllable answers, giggling, using too many hand gestures and smoking too much. You should not smoke at all unless the interviewer positively invites you to do so.

If you are not sure whether or not you are guilty of these or any other irritating mannerisms ask someone you know really well to tell you and consciously work to stop yourself when doing your mock interview (see p. 61).

Giving a good impression

To sum up, positive body language that will give a good impression includes:

- dressing smartly and appropriately;
- walking and sitting with good posture;
- shaking hands firmly and briefly;
- relaxed behaviour;
- looking at the interviewer as you speak to each other;
- smiling when you arrive and leave and where appropriate during the interview;
- speaking clearly and loudly enough to be heard;
- judging when you have said enough.

More detailed information about body language can be found in several books listed at the end.

Coping with nerves and stress

Nervousness is not a sign of inadequacy on your part. We are all of us at the mercy of our adrenaline, and there is a very fine dividing line between being justifiably keyed up and ready to do your best and being rendered helpless by panic. There are steps you can take to counter the effects of nervousness but try not to get worked up about staying calm along with everything else. Sometimes the harder you try to stay calm the more difficult it becomes. The interviewer will expect you to be slightly nervous, indeed may be rather alienated if you are so laid back that you appear almost indifferent.

It is quite normal for an interview to have periods of awkwardness, especially when problem questions are being discussed. It will be the same for all the other candidates so do not allow tricky moments to throw you off balance. They happen in all interviews.

Keeping a sense of proportion

The *first step*—and most important step—towards controlling nerves is in your mental attitude. Nervousness and its symptoms are the result of fear. It stands to reason that if you can eradicate the fear the nervousness will subside. Do not just skip over this bit. Really think about it. Imagine the very worst that can happen at the interview—you fall over, give all the wrong answers, blush and become tongue-tied, antagonize the interviewer, do everything so badly you patently have not got a hope of getting the job. Does it honestly really matter? Your biggest fear is probably the fear of making a fool of yourself and this is what is making you nervous. Do everything you can to avoid mishaps by being adequately prepared but ask yourself again—does it *really* matter? Even if everything does go wrong the interviewer will have forgotten the disasters which seem so catastrophic to you five minutes after you have left the room. In the final analysis you are getting nervous and undermining your chances for success because you are frightened of something which really does not matter as much as you are allowing it to.

This then becomes further complicated because you get frightened of displaying the symptoms of nervousness and being embarrassed by them so you add another layer of fear and resultant nervousness to the situation.

Try to counter nervousness by getting right back to basics. What are you trying to achieve? What is the worst that can happen if you do not achieve it? Is that really so bad when you look at it in perspective?

Adequate preparation reduces stress

An important contribution to staying calm is arriving at the interview conscious that you have done everything you can to be thoroughly well prepared. You can then realistically reassure yourself that you have nothing to worry about. The more care you have taken in your application, gathering background information, knowing what questions you want to ask, preparing yourself to counter any awkward questions, ensuring that you are suitably dressed and that you arrive unflustered in good time for your appointment, the less reason you will have to be nervous and the more confident you will feel.

Positive thinking

Think positive! Every interview is valuable experience and good practice, so look on it as time well spent even if you are not hopeful about the outcome. Better still, be positive about yourself and your own good qualities. You are a worthwhile person so why *should* you be nervous?

Getting the interviewer in perspective

Remember the interviewer wants you to do well. Hostile interviewers are few and far between. The person you are about to see is probably a rather harassed individual who is hoping that the ideal employee is going to be, as we have mentioned before, the next person to walk through the door. That person ought to be you.

It has sometimes been suggested that if you feel easily intimidated by an interviewer, and therefore are paralysed by nerves, you should imagine him/her in a ludicrous situation, such as sitting in the Albert Hall with no clothes on. This approach certainly helps you realize that you are dealing with another fallible human being. If it is a technique which works for you then by all means use it.

Physical effects of nervousness

The *second step* is controlling the actual physical effects on you of all the adrenaline which is produced when you sense you are in a threatening situation. These include pounding heart, dry mouth, stiff face muscles, sweaty palms, tension in the neck and shoulders, a desire to go to the lavatory and the feeling that sitting calmly is a great strain and you would rather be pacing up and down the room. These are all responses which were highly suitable in prehistoric times when events required either that you ran away as fast as you could or that you had a surge of energy to help you fight your way out of a difficult situation as ferociously as possible (fight or flight behaviour). Unfortunately the mental stresses we have to deal with nowadays usually require less physical solutions. The effects of the adrenaline which prepared us for a fight or flight situation actually work against us when we cannot do either. However, since we are keyed up for decisive physical action this is still the best way of working it off.

Walking works off tension

One of the simplest things to do is to work off some of the tension by walking to the interview if at all possible. A brisk walk will help use up the adrenaline which creates the physical manifestations of nervousness. If, when you arrive at the interview you find you are early or there is a delay, don't just sit around allowing tension to build up inside you. Use the extra time to go for a walk around the block, or even just round the building. Obviously you should check with the receptionist or whoever is organizing the candidates that you are not going to miss your turn if you are out for a while. Walking around worrying about whether or not you are going to be late will be counterproductive.

Relaxing tense muscles

As well as using up adrenaline you may also need to relax muscles which have stiffened up because of tension. This is very important for facial muscles. It is unnerving to want to smile at the interviewer only to discover that your face has set and feels too stiff to move. Loosen up facial muscles by stretching your whole face and trying to move the muscles up and down and from side to side. Silent yawning will also bring back mobility to your face.

You will probably find that once the interview is under way you will start to relax. The worst moment always seems to be immediately before you step into the unknown. Pulling a few exaggerated grimaces just before you go through the door will help you make the first important smile.

Tension in the neck and shoulders can be eased by circling the shoulders up and around a few times backwards and forwards and by circling your head slowly down to your chest and then up so that your neck is stretched with your chin in the air.

Tension in the hands and feet can be eased by alternately stretching and clenching fingers and toes half a dozen times.

You can restore a more relaxed feeling to your body by flopping forward, dangling your arms in front of you and shaking your hands loosely from the wrists.

All these tension-releasing exercises are effective. But if there is someone else waiting with you, and you feel shy doing some of the more noticeable ones, disappear to the cloakroom for a few minutes and do them there.

Deep breathing

One exercise that you can do anywhere is deep breathing. Holding your breath builds up tension and shallow breathing denies your body the oxygen it needs to function at maximum efficiency. Taking controlled deep breaths will calm you down and get you into a more relaxed rhythm rather than a state of uncontrolled panic.

Needing the loo

If you are the sort of person who needs to go to the lavatory when you are nervous make sure you know where it is. This will take the edge off your anxiety. Often when you know it is possible the need seems to wear off. Similarly, remind yourself that even if the worst comes to the worst and you need to go in the middle of the interview it is no big deal although it feels like a disaster to you. After all, interviewers are human too. It is only common sense not to drink large quantities of diuretic liquid like coffee or fruit juice before an interview. If you find your throat is dry and you need some water just take a few sips to moisten your mouth.

Shaky hands

You may be someone whose hands shake when they are nervous. The exercise to clench and unclench your hands will help to relieve the muscle tension which causes this. Let your hands lie loosely in your lap, palms upward, during the interview or clasp them lightly together. Do not accept offers of tea or coffee if this is your problem as you will then give yourself the further anxiety of controlling the cup and saucer. Instead, if your mouth is feeling dry think of sucking a really juicy lemon. This trick soon gets the saliva flowing again.

Act calm—stay calm

One successful method of mastering nerves is to act the way you would like to feel. This is a means of working backwards towards the state you would like to achieve. Instead of feeling nervous and so acting nervously, act calmly and you will trick yourself into feeling calm. Behave in a confident and deliberate fashion. Move. your body deliberately and comparatively slowly, not in the over-hasty, potentially clumsy way of someone who is a mass of nerves. Smile at the receptionist, sit calmly without fidgeting in the waiting room. Pick up something to read and look at it carefully, not frantically flicking through the pages. When your turn comes to go in, gather up your possessions slowly and deliberately. Knock on

43

the door, and when called enter calmly and confidently with a smile. When invited to sit down take your time, make sure you are comfortable, place your bag or briefcase carefully by your side. Control nervous gestures such as foot-tapping or twisting your fingers together. When asked a question do not rush at your answer but give yourself a second or two to compose your thoughts. This does not mean you should behave like an automaton. You may feel you are moving very slowly, but in fact you will simply be counteracting a nervous tendency to rush headlong into everything and to lose control of what is going on. Anyone with experience of public speaking knows that when you stand up you should not speak absolutely immediately. A few seconds' pause gives the speaker a chance to calm down and gauge the atmosphere in the room. The short silence encourages the audience to take notice and concentrate. Like a public speaker you should give yourself a chance to collect your thoughts and your audience a chance to collect theirs. Act the way you would like to behave and the chances are the act and the real thing will merge.

Learning relaxation technique

At the back of the book there is a list of courses run to help people with interview technique. These courses always cover the problem of controlling unnecessary nervousness. Courses on public speaking, which are often available cheaply at night school are also good places for learning the techniques of relaxing when dealing with other people. You may also find more general classes in the techniques of relaxation helpful. Many of these techniques culminate in your being able to trigger off a general sense of relaxation when it suits you. This usually requires quite a lot of practice but is invaluable once it has been mastered.

The form of the interview

There is a generally accepted standard interview format which goes something like this:

- Handshake and greeting (possibly following a short tour of the work place)
- General chitchat to relax the candidate and establish rapport
- A brief summary by the interviewee about herself/himself
- Home background
- Educational background and qualifications

- Why are you changing your job/applying for this particular job?
- What sort of job do you want?
- A look at the job on offer and/or the company
- Terms and conditions
- Opportunity for the interviewee to ask additional questions
- Thank you and goodbye (including when and how the candidate should hear the outcome; details of interview expenses)

Of course these headings cover more than one question and it may not always be clear to you how the interviewer is constructing the interview. All interviewers are different. Some are well prepared and have taken the trouble to find out how to conduct a selection interview, especially if they are highly trained personnel officers. Others may surprise you by being woefully unprepared and you may find yourself taking the initiative more often than you might have expected in order to be able to put across as many of your good points as possible.

An interview is a conversation between equals

Whatever category your interviewer falls into you should remind yourself even at this late stage that an interview is basically a conversation to find out how well two sides of a potential deal might suit one another.

It is a conversation between equals, even if you are applying for a relatively humble post. The employer is offering money and/or status. You are offering your time and probably your expertise. Even if you are hoping to work in a subordinate position for the very person who is interviewing you, you do not need to take a passive role in the interview. Indeed it will probably be harmful, for at the very least the interviewer will expect you to take a positive interest in the job on offer and in the company. Moreover you genuinely need to find out at this stage whether or not the job will suit you. You will therefore be expected to ask questions as well as answer them.

Breaking the ice

The preliminary chat which usually prefaces the interview proper is intended to break the ice and give both sides a chance to size each other up. It gives the interviewee a useful chance to hear the sound of his or her own voice in this artificial situation, without starting immediately on important subjects. Keep your replies brief but as relaxed and friendly as possible. This stage is intended mainly to ease the initial awkwardness, the interviewer does not really want your detailed impressions of the weather or the route you took to get to the interview. Now is a good moment to emphasize that however friendly and informal the interviewer is being you should not fall into the trap of overfamiliarity. This causes antagonism towards you faster than almost anything else. Take your cue from the tone set by the interviewer but err on the side of formality. The interviewer may address you by your first name, especially if you are a young person. This is done to help you relax. Even if the interviewer is using your first name she/he will not expect you to return the compliment unless you are specifically asked to do so.

Telling the interviewer about yourself

Serious questioning will probably begin with the time-honoured phrase, 'Tell me about yourself'. Do not respond by an endless recitation of your life from your earliest years. A couple of minutes should be quite adequate to summarize the following points about yourself:

- profession/occupation;
- main areas of experience/expertise;
- main skills and qualities.

The interviewer will then ask more detailed questions about your background/education/experience. The more high-powered the job the more detailed these questions will be and the better prepared you will need to be to answer them.

The interviewer will be looking for:

- a good standard of 'spoken English'—accents do not matter but sloppy speech does;
- simple answers to questions;
- a confident nature, not too reserved but not too arrogant;
- a clear record of personal development;
- a good grasp of the facts;
- examples given from experience to back up answers;
- someone who:
  has initiative,
  presents solutions to problems,
  pays attention to detail,
  has ability to isolate the important detail,
  works well under pressure,

46

sees the job through,
has the ability to meet deadlines.

Keep answers informative but not too long

A good interviewer will help you through the interview so that you concentrate on the areas she/he needs to know about and do not ramble. For example the interviewer may preface a clutch of questions with a general phrase such as, 'I'd like to talk a little about your home background', or 'Let's take a look at the sort of experience you have had in the retail business', so that you will find yourself keeping your answers to the subsequent questions pertinent to the area in which the interviewer is interested and do not wander off the point.

Try not to to give one-word answers even if the interviewer is inexperienced and keeps phrasing questions so that the most obvious way to answer is 'Yes' or 'No'.

While it is important to avoid monosyllabic answers do not make the mistake of rambling on interminably and losing the interviewer's interest. Talking too much has the additional disadvantage that you may end up revealing more than you intended, especially if you do not want to draw attention to a lack of relevant expertise, or a past unhappy work experience. Nervousness affects people in different ways. While some people become tongue-tied others cannot stop talking. Be aware of the category you fall into before you go for the interview and make a conscious effort to avoid the pitfalls.

Typical interview questions

Think about questions in advance

The interviewee has to assume that all the questions an interviewer asks are asked with a reason, although some may seem irrelevant and some unnecessarily personal. The following questions are among the commonest used in interviews (p. 48). Go through them to see which might be relevant to your own situation. Work out approximately how you would answer them. Do *not* try to learn specific answers parrot-fashion. You cannot expect to be asked the questions exactly as they appear here and you will be badly thrown if you have programmed yourself with exact responses to very particular questions which do not crop up in the way you had anticipated. On the other hand, if a question is asked exactly as it appears here and you give an answer which has clearly been prepared in advance and learned off by heart you will not be very convincing.

Be prepared for problem questions

Use the questions simply as a guideline. Take particular trouble with any which might present you with difficulties and have a credible reply worked out to sidestep problem areas. Try and understand what the interviewer will be hoping to find out by asking the questions, so that your replies can be relevant and informative.

Practise out loud

An invaluable exercise is to practise saying your answers out loud. Ideally this should be as part of a 'mock interview' set up with a friend or colleague. However it is also valuable to practise out loud by yourself, and it is even better if you can tape record your answers so that you can hear how you sound. If you are not happy with any of the answers do not despair. The second attempt is always much better than the first and *any* experience of hearing your answers voiced out loud will make the eventual interview an easier and more constructive experience.

Devising appropriate answers to typical questions

Under the first few sample questions are guidelines to help you understand what the interviewer is hoping to find out so that you can construct replies which show why you are the candidate who should get the job. Wherever possible try to angle your answer so that it is clearly relevant to the job for which you are applying.

Jot down on paper answers which you think adequately cover all the points. Practise speaking your answers out loud but do not learn them off by heart.

Sample questions

How would you describe your home background?

This usually crops up when fairly young people and school-leavers apply for jobs, because the interviewer has little or no work record by which to judge the calibre of the applicants. It is often asked when a firm is taking on people for training when a lot of money will be wasted if the trainee does not have what it takes to stay the course. If you understand the reason why the question is being asked you will feel less inclined to regard the interviewer as unduly poking his or her nose into your private business. You should indicate the aspects of your background which the interviewer is looking for without rambling on about things which are irrelevant. Points to stress include stability, an encouraging and positive attitude to education, parents or relatives who have been involved in similar work, and an enthusiastic attitude to hard work. Try and pick out the aspects of your background which make you especially suitable for the job you have applied for.

Never include the negative aspects of your home background.

Why did you study (x) subjects at school/college?

Make your answer a constructive one. Obviously if you did a course in engineering or modern languages and you are going for a job where these skills are required it should not be difficult to explain that this is what positively interests you and you chose the subject because you wanted to go on to employment in the same field. If you are talking about more general studies or if you did a non-vocational course at college or university you should show how this demonstrates that you are capable of becoming interested in a wide range of subjects and could bring the same enthusiasm to your work. You could also bring up the point that learning how to study any subject successfully makes you quicker at learning new skills and better able to handle the unfamiliar skills you will have to learn as part of the job.

Never say you do not know why you picked certain subjects, or that other people decided for you, as this will show you in a negative light.

What did you do in your last job?

Here the interviewer is basically looking to find out two things. First, how far the skills and experience acquired and used in your last job match up to those necessary to the new job, so that the transition will be relatively simple and there will not be too much disruption while you learn the ropes. Second, how successful you were in the last job so that she/he can gauge what calibre of person you are. Your reply should therefore include not just what you actually did but any special skills you were able to bring to the job and any particular equipment you have been trained to use.

Demonstrate the type of person you are by referring to any special responsibilities you had and any promotion which you earned. Try to round off your answer by demonstrating how the old job has fitted you to take on the job you are applying for. For example, if they are both jobs which require an ability to get on well with people point this out. If the new job represents a step up the ladder, point out how it is a logical progression from the job before.

Do not simply give a list of the work you have been doing up to date but show how the experience you have gained in the other job has *directly* fitted you to do the new one.

Have you done this kind of work before?

This can be a tricky one if you haven't! If you are going for a job that you have never done before, either from necessity or because you are looking for a change of direction, you should take care to prepare for this question by listing all the experience and personal qualities you have which suit you for the job. Begin your reply positively with the word *yes*, and then go on to describe the most relevant experience you have. Bring in related work experience with the emphasis on how quick you are to learn new skills. If you have any non-work experience that is relevant, a hobby perhaps, mention this. Work out beforehand the sort of person you think would be most suitable for the job and tell the interviewer which personal qualities you have which you feel would suit you to the job.

Never answer this question with a straight *no*, or you will lose the interviewer's interest immediately.

Why did you leave your last job?

It is vital to prepare a way round this question well before the interview itself. The interviewer is trying to find out if you left your last job for reasons which could pose similar problems if you came to work with his/her firm. For example, if you left because of a poor relationship with your boss or poor work performance it is going to put a lot of doubts in the mind of the interviewer if you come straight out with it.

If there *was* some difficulty involved which resulted in your leaving a job, avoid referring to it, but do not resort to outright lying as this will rebound badly against you if you are found out. Instead, place the emphasis on the more straightforward reasons for leaving, after all few decisions are the result of just one factor but are usually the result of a combination of circumstances.

Some reasons you may find apply in your case include: deciding on a career change; looking for more responsibility (both good, positive reasons); coming to the end of seasonal or short-contract employment; insufficient money; wanting to work closer to home.

If the reason was redundancy do not say that you were made redundant but that the *job itself* became redundant. There is a subtle but very real difference in where you place the emphasis, and the interviewer will not then automatically make the assumption that there was something lacking in you which caused you to be made redundant.

If the reason for leaving was ill-health refer to it briefly, explain it was a temporary situation and emphasize your present fitness and ability to take on the demands of the new job.

Never run down or criticize a past employer, even if you have to refer to disagreements. Explain the problem if you must as a difference in approach to the job; if you denigrate a previous boss the interviewer will assume that you will do the same thing next time around.

Why do you want to work with this company?

The interviewer is looking for a positive and enthusiastic approach to his or her company. This will show that you are genuinely interested in this particular job as opposed to any old job. If you can show genuine enthusiasm for the company the interviewer will be reassured that you will stay a reasonable time with the firm and not be constantly on the lookout for something better. If, as suggested, you have done some background work on the company you will be in a good position to say what you really like about it, why you think it has a reputation as a good employer, why the job suits you ideally. Signs that you have gone to some trouble to find out about the firm will be very much in your favour.

Never say that there are no particular reasons why you want to work with the company.

What do you think are your weaknesses/failings?

It is hard to know why interviewers persist in using this question. If you are silly enough to categorize all your faults for the interviewer you will surely already have shown yourself as unsuitable for the job in many other ways. Once again the key to this question is to apply positive thinking. Do not say, 'I do not have any weaknesses at all', as this will be patently untrue. Instead reply along the lines of, 'I don't think I have any weaknesses which would affect my ability to do this job'. If pressed to think of something then be prepared with a 'weakness' which can also be interpreted as a point in your favour. For example, you could say, 'I find I tend to get very involved in my work', or 'I like to see things move along quickly'.

Never tell an interviewer any of your failings. You should be aware of your own weaknesses if you have done a thorough self-assessment but the information is for your own eyes only.

How would you change things if you came here?

This question is often given to people applying for a job in management or administration. The interviewer is looking to see if you have real experience of a similar situation enough to be aware of where possible areas for attention lie. She/he is also looking for initiative and indications that you have given some thought to what the job will involve.

However, you should also make it clear that you would not expect to come in and immediately start changing things for the sake of it. Explain that you would need time to make a thorough assessment of the situation and would be aware of the dangers of treading on other people's toes. Efficient management includes knowing how to handle people as well as organizing a smooth-running machine.

If you are unsure of what you might change or there is clearly no *one* correct answer then place the emphasis on doing nothing until you are thoroughly familiar with the set up.

*   *   *

Dealing with aggressive interviewers

If you are confronted with an aggressively rude interviewer who makes the interview very stressful you may want to ask yourself whether you could possibly be happy working in such an atmosphere anyway.

If you want the job despite this experience then you must stay calm. Do not allow the interviewer to rile you. Do not apologize as your weaknesses, failings and gaps in your c.v. are thrown at you. Give the most positive explanations you can and try to keep control of what you want to put over during the interview rather than being forced into a purely defensive position. Take your own advantage of the difficult atmosphere by realizing that things cannot get much worse so it is worth while going out on a limb to say what you want to say without worrying about causing a negative reaction!

Bringing it to an end

If things are really bad, you are getting nowhere and you feel that an argument is developing, the best action is to state politely that you are not willing to be interviewed in such a manner, that you are clearly wasting one another's time and you have decided to leave. Gather up your belongings and make calmly for the door. However, we should emphasize that this stalemate is highly unlikely.

Awkward questions

Sometimes even well-meaning interviewers will throw you a really awkward question. This will probably be to see if you can think on your feet and react well under stress. If you can recognize these for what they are you are well on the way to coping with them. Typically such questions begin with, 'What would you do if . . .', and then create a hypothetical situation which it is hard for the candidate to imagine. The most important thing is to stay calm, give yourself time to think and *ask for clarification* if necessary. Don't try and answer something you do not understand in the hope that you can work it out as you go along. If you do you will become muddled and make a bad impression.

Another typical 'stress' technique is to say, 'Sell yourself to me'. Try and work this one out before the interview. Your aim should be to emphasize your goods points without sounding boastful.

The interviewer may try to catch you out (or simply be thoughtless) by asking questions directly related to the job description or advertisement which brought you to the interview. If you cannot remember the details and do not have the relevant piece of paper in front of you, you may find yourself floundering as you try to answer a question you have not really understood. Rather than trying to bluff your way through, it is better to say something like, 'Right at this moment it's rather difficult to remember the exact details, could I possibly look over the advertisement again?' If the interviewer was merely asking the question without thinking that should present no problem. If it was said in the hope of catching you out you will at least have demonstrated a calm approach and an ability not to panic. However, it is always wise to remind yourself of the job description details before an interview and also to be thoroughly conversant with the details of your own application form and c.v.

The most stressful thing the interviewer can do is simply to let silence fall after you think you have answered a question. This is a very old trick, and one often used by journalists. The awkwardness will probably prompt you to talk just for the sake of filling in the space, and you may say more than you wanted to or even find yourself talking rubbish. If you are aware of this you can avoid the pitfalls. Do not feel it is up to you to keep filling the silence if you have nothing more you want to say. If the interviewer remains silent then look at her or him as if you are expecting the next move to come from their side. If there is no response it is best to say something like, 'I don't think there is anything more I can add to my answer', and place the ball firmly back in the interviewer's court.

Classic examples of awkward questions are the salesman's special dread, as the interviewer picks up the telephone directory and says, 'Sell me this', and the totally unpredictable, 'What star sign are you?' The first presents the candidate with an unreal situation, and probably the most that will be learned is whether or not the candidate is good-natured enough to play silly games. The second is a nightmare—how do you know whether or not the interviewer feels incompatible with your sign or believes that people born under your sign are genetically hopeless at the job? The truth is there is only so much preparation you can do. Do the best you can, hope for the best with the unpredictable and try to keep a sense of humour.

Below are some rather more typical questions that you should be prepared to encounter. Look at them with a view to:

- what the interviewer is trying to discover
- what your reply should reveal about your positive qualities
- what you should definitely *avoid* saying

There are further questions in the section for interviewers if you would like more practice at this exercise.

Some typical interview questions

- What do you think are your greatest strengths? (Be positive but avoid boasting)
- What interests do you have outside work? (Be sure to have some!)
- What was your previous employer's opinion of you?
- What attracted you to this particular job?
- Why should we hire you instead of one of the other candidates?
- Do you regard yourself as ambitious? (Interviewers like a certain amount of ambition)
- How important to you think qualifications are?

- Why have you been in your last job for such a long time? (Emphasize diversity of work experience within that one job, and the fact that you enjoyed your job.)
- Why have you had so many jobs in the last few years? (Emphasize trying to gain wide experience quickly. Show they followed on logically but make it clear you are ready to settle down.)
- Do you regard yourself to the left or to the right in politics? (Best to avoid extremes)
- How would you bridge the gap between management and workers?
- How often were you absent from your previous job?
- What is your health like?
- What arrangement have you made for the children if they are ill or on holiday?
- How old are you?
- What machines and equipment are you familiar with?
- What sort of salary are you looking for?
- When would you be available to start?

Be prepared for technical questions

Some jobs require a high level of technical or theoretical expertise. If you are working in a very technical field you should do your homework before the interview so that you are prepared for detailed questions about equipment and techniques you may have to deal with.

Listen carefully to the questions

Whatever the job is, however humble or high-powered, you must make a positive effort to listen to the interviewer and answer the questions he or she actually puts to you. When you are nervous and anxious to please it is too easy to only half-listen and to leap in with an answer which is not quite relevant. It is perfectly in order to pause before answering a question so that you can be totally sure you have understood what has been said to you and to give some thought to your answer. It is also perfectly in order to say, 'May I think about that for a moment?' before answering a question, although clearly it would become rather tedious if you said that every time.

Questioning the interviewer

Towards the closing stages of the interview the interviewer will probably ask you if *you* have any questions you want to ask. There are two important points to remember about this.

First, the interviewer will be expecting questions related to the company and what the job involves. Straightforward queries on pay, working conditions, etc., can be answered by your own information-gathering *prior* to the interview. Only ask questions on these topics if there is something you are genuinely unsure of and need to clarify. It will alienate the interviewer if you seem mainly concerned to ensure your holiday will not have to be cancelled or that you will be eligible for the next pay rise.

Second, you should try and incorporate your questions into the interview as it goes along and not leave them all to the end. If you have been successful in treating the interview as a two-way communication then much of what you hope to say will arise naturally as part of the interchange between you. You should not feel that it is presumptuous to ask. The interviewer will expect to answer pertinent questions.

There is no need to ask questions at this stage just for the sake of it. If you have made your queries part of the interview and done your background research thoroughly the answer to the interviewer's question may well be 'No, you have already explained everything very thoroughly thank you'. This does not mean you are lacking in initiative—just well organized. If you want to make the point you can add that you have already spoken to the Personnel Department about pay and conditions.

Below is a selection of questions you might like to ask, either during the interview or when invited to do so by the interviewer. You can ask them either just as they are or use them as a basis for formulating questions that are particularly related to the job for which you are being interviewed.

Some questions to ask the interviewer

- How did the vacancy arise? (If this is the result of company expansion then the chances of career opportunities are good)
- Can you give me a more exact picture of what the job involves? (You are not just at the interview to see if you suit the company but to see if the job genuinely suits you)
- How will my work be monitored?

- Who will assess my work?
- When will I become eligible for further training?
- When will I be given some responsibility?
- Who will be responsible to me?
- Add your own questions to the list whenever any occur to you. (Keep specific questions for specific jobs in your interview file (see p. 30))

Additional points if you are redundant or long-term unemployed

Going for interview is always unsettling even if you are employed and looking to change or improve your job. If you have been made redundant or have been unemployed for a long time you have two additional problems to overcome.

The first is that you have probably developed a very poor self-image which is reflected in your performance during interviews. This is hardly surprising as it takes a very buoyant personality indeed to cope with what appears to be constant rejection.

The second problem is the prejudice which redundancy and long-term unemployment may create in the mind of the interviewer. Twenty years ago, during a period of full employment, employers may sometimes have been right to assume that those who were unemployed or redundant were less effective than those who held down a job. As unemployment began to escalate it may also have been true that those who were the first to be made redundant or were turned down for work were those who were least efficient.

Nowadays, with unemployment at an appallingly high level, it is far more likely that people who have been unable to find work are simply the victims of economic and political circumstances.

However, if you have been made redundant or are long-term unemployed you need to understand the thinking behind the interviewer's prejudices and strive to overcome them by demonstrating strongly that you are unemployed because of circumstances beyond your control, not because you yourself are inadequate.

Applying method to job applications

Initially the aim is to get called for interview, and this is the hardest part. There are no easy answers but if you have not already been applying all the techniques listed in this book when applying for jobs you should find that a methodical approach is more productive than previous haphazard applications. Even so, you may find yourself writing hundreds of letters and sending out hundreds of c.v.s on the offchance of a response. This is not unusual and does not mean that you are a greater failure than anyone else.

Forming self-help groups

If you know of others in the same situation you might find it helpful to team up, especially if you are not in direct competition for the same jobs. This will keep you going when you might be tempted to give up. You can compare notes, practise 'mock interviews', advise and criticize each other's c.v.s, ask around for jobs and training schemes for both of you. You may find the competitive element useful for stirring you on to greater efforts, and you will certainly find it reassuring to know that you share a common problem and that there is not something intrinsically wrong with *you*. If there are enough of you, you can make up a more formal self-help group. You will undoubtedly find strength and reassurance in numbers and you will be able to ask for assistance from agencies, training schemes and counsellors to help your particular group.

Being organized leads to confidence

Settling down to approach the problem in an organized fashion, alone or with someone else, will help you reassess your own attitude and if you are more positive this will come over in your applications. It will certainly be reflected in your performance if you reach an interview.

Take up training opportunities

Increased confidence can also be the result of using time when unemployed to acquire new skills. This is particularly important for people in the older age group who encounter much prejudice about their ability to adapt to new working methods and/or the stresses of high pressure production methods or computerized management skills.

If you are made redundant try to get some sort of retraining as fast as possible, before you lose your nerve. If you have been unemployed for a while seek retraining as a first step to a new, positive attitude.

At best, training may open new avenues or provide contacts which may lead to employment interviews. At the very least, the discipline of being involved in some form of training will help counteract the feeling of lethargy that creeps over many people who have been unemployed for a long while—a characteristic which is very counterproductive in an interview.

Voluntary work

The same is true of voluntary work, much of which involves concrete skills such as typing, driving, accountancy or teaching others technical skills. Voluntary work can provide a framework for job-seeking and will make a favourable impression at an interview.

Interviewers are looking for enthusiasm and initiative

Although if you are redundant or long-term unemployed you feel you have heard all of this before, the truth is that if you manage to keep alive some enthusiasm and initiative you have more chance of getting an interview than if you do not. And if you get an interview you are more likely to succeed if you can prove that you are a positive person who has made demonstrable efforts to counteract the ill-effects of being unemployed and have managed to put your time to constructive use. Interviewers are looking for qualities like confidence and ambition. If you lose these you will put yourself at an even greater disadvantage.

Dealing with questions about age—older candidates

Anyone over the age of 50, and in some fields over the age of 45 (younger for women), should have given a lot of thought to answering an interviewer's question about age. There is a great deal of prejudice about age, with the result that the older you are the more likely you are to remain unemployed for more than a year. You are also far less likely to be taken on for training. This is because older people are assumed to be less flexible, less motivated and more 'tired' than those in their 20s and early 30s.

It is up to you positively to counter these opinions. As with redundancy, do not bring up the subject yourself but if it is discussed do not lie. Instead try to emphasize the positive aspects of your age. These may include experience, a more equable disposition, more settled way of life, less tendency to want to chop and change, no demands from a young family (women's work record *improves* as they get older), proven ability and reliability, a number of good references, willingness to work unsocial hours. There is a growing awareness among employers of prejudice towards older people. In the United States there is even legislation to combat it. Although changes in attitude are notoriously slow there are now some firms and local governments which positively avoid specifying age in their job advertisements. It helps you take up a positive attitude if you are aware that others have recognized that age discrimination exists and is unfair.

Dealing with questions about age—younger candidates

Another distinct group among the long-term unemployed are the very young, many of whom have never had a chance to prove themselves in a job. If this applies be prepared to show the interviewer what the advantages of your youth are. These may include ability to learn easily, familiarity with new technology such as computers, no demanding family ties, willingness to travel, willingness to work, plenty of energy.

To summarize: if you have been made redundant or have been unemployed for a long period:

- make every effort to retrain as soon as possible
- adopt a methodical approach to job applications
- team up with others in the same position
- use voluntary work to 'shape' your day, keep skills sharp and demonstrate to the interviewer that you have used your time constructively
- consciously work towards a positive attitude about yourself
- be confident about yourself in interviews
- be prepared with positive and well-reasoned responses for negative questions about your age, why you were made redundant, why you have been out of work so long, whether you have lost skills through lack of use, whether you have failed to keep in touch with your original skills
- be thorough in your preparation for the interview and in applying for jobs

It is clear that those who are in employment have less difficulty being called for interview and being successful than those who are without work. However, as time goes by and the problem of unemployment does not seem to diminish more thought is being given to the specific problems of those applying for work while out of a job.

Jobclubs

One of the most interesting new schemes to be put forward is the

Jobclubs which are now being set up at Job Centres. Their aim is to teach people common-sense techniques of job application and interview performance like the ones in this book. Much of the work is practical, including 'mock' interviews and advice on completing application forms and preparing c.v.s. Jobclubs are aimed at the younger and less skilled end of the market.

Professional and executive recruitment

Those who are older and who are looking for managerial and executive jobs can also get valuable advice from the Manpower Services Commission's Professional and Executive Recruitment. Their booklet, *The Job Hunting Handbook*, is clear and full of useful advice. They also produce a newspaper, *Executive Post*. Details of all these services are given at the end of the book.

Mock interviews

In the run-up to the interview, or even before if you have the time, it is a good idea to try a few practice interviews. These are an integral part of the professional courses which are run for people trying to improve their chances of getting a job. Although you may not want to go on a course, or cannot afford to, it is a good idea to ask a friend or relative you feel comfortable with to play the part of the interviewer and let you have a dummy run. This will enable them to point out any of your obvious failings (you don't need to be a professional counsellor to realize when someone is mumbling or unprepared for certain questions). It will also give you the opportunity to get used to hearing the sound of your own voice and to work out a way of expressing clearly the points you would like to put across.

Use a tape-recorder

It is particularly useful if you tape-record the whole session so that you can hear your performance yourself. If you cannot find someone to conduct a mock interview then leave a tape-recorder on while you practise some of your more important answers and the way in which you describe yourself to the interviewer. You will probably be surprised at what a different experience it is actually speaking the words rather than running through them in your head.

Mock interviews and tape-recording answers will pay handsome dividends at the interview itself when you would otherwise find yourself practising your answers for the first time.

Setting the scene

Take a little trouble setting the situation properly. Your 'interviewer' should sit behind a desk or table so that you can get the feel of approaching someone in a 'dominant' situation. You yourself should go out of the room. This will enable you to practise from the moment when you are called. Entering the room in a confident and relaxed manner is very important for getting the interview off to a good start.

Look at the sections on the form of the interview from both points of view (pp. 44 and 94) to see the shape the interview is normally expected to take. The 'interviewer' should use some of the questions suggested for interviewers in that section. You should also let the 'interviewer' know what particular questions might be a problem for you—'What arrangements have you made for your children out of school hours?', 'Why have you had three different jobs in the last twelve months?', 'Why were you made redundant?', etc., so that you can practise positive responses to them.

Keep it spontaneous

However, you should not work out the entire mock interview beforehand or you will lose the element of spontaneity. The real interview may run a very different course from the one you anticipated, and you do not want to develop the subconscious belief that it can only go one way.

Practise your own questions

Finally, the 'interviewer' should ask you if you have any questions of your own (this usually, though not always, comes towards the end of the interview). There are some suggestions to prompt you on pp. 56–7.

Making a smooth exit

You should practise saying goodbye, thanking the interviewer, shaking his/her hand if it is proffered and making a confident exit. It is usual for an interviewer to show the candidate to the door with a few final words. Sometimes you have to make your own way out. Practise both ways.

The following checklist will help the 'interviewer' be of genuine help to you. Add to it any points that you may be particularly anxious to get right and discuss it together.

Checklist for mock interviews

		√ or X
1	Confident entrance into room (not peering round door)	
2	Handshake and greeting	
3	If a woman, did she place her handbag down sensibly (not on interviewer's desk or clutching it on her lap)?	
4	Sitting posture good, not slouched	
5	Appearance good, clean and tidy	
6	Kept still, without irritating nervous mannerisms (such as hand over mouth, twisting and untwisting legs)	
7	Polite and confident manner	
8	Friendly but not overfamiliar in speech and mannerisms	
9	Speech clear and loud enough	
10	Looked at the interviewer, kept eye contact	
11	Gave good answers to questions about: Last job Qualifications and skills Health Any problem questions	
12	'Sold himself/herself' well without bragging	
13	Did not go on too long	
14	Not 'thrown' by probing questions	
15	Showed keen interest in the job/company	
16	Smiled occasionally, when appropriate	
17	Realized when interview coming to an end	

General remarks about interviewee's behaviour and manner:

_____

_____

Answers to questions:_____

_____

Interview follow-up

Reviewing your performance

Every interview can be a useful and constructive experience and doing a proper interview follow-up will help you get the most out of it, even if you are not successful in getting the job. As soon as you arrive home, or between interviews (if you have more than one in a day), and while the interview is still fresh in your mind, head a piece of paper with the date, place and name of the job you were applying for. Then add the following checklist and go through it to see how you rate your performance. When you see how you have marked it, think about the answers you gave and pinpoint the ones where your answers were weakest.

Post-interview checklist

√ or X

1	Punctuality	
2	Appearance	
3	Entrance confident	
4	Shook hands	
5	Kept good posture	
6	Controlled nervous mannerisms	
7	Listened to interviewer	
8	Answered questions fully with reference to the job	
9	'Sold' myself without boasting	

10	Managed to bring in
	    qualifications
	    previous experience
	    personal interests	

11	Were my qualifications suitable? If not, why not?	
12	Pointed out my special strengths	
13	Able to cope with questions about weaknesses	
14	Demonstrated how I was suited to the job	
15	Gave references	
16	Was able to ask my own questions	
17	Looked at interviewer while talking	
18	Smiled	
19	Thanks and handshake at end	

Questions I should rethink or practise:

- about last job;
- previous jobs;
- reasons for leaving;
- qualifications;
- health;
- age;
- my personal circumstances;
- my future plans/career;
- others.

Before the next interview get to work on any weaknesses shown up on your checklist. If the main stumbling block is how you present yourself try to find someone who will practise mock interviews with you, concentrating on any problem areas the checklist has helped to reveal.

Follow-up letter

A good way of emphasizing your interest in the job and of keeping your image fresh in the mind of the interviewer is to write a follow-up letter after the interview. Evidence of your continuing enthusiasm may possibly tip the balance in your favour if the interviewer is having difficulty coming to a decision out of a large number of applicants. You must gauge for yourself whether or not you have struck up a good relationship with the interviewer and whether a letter would work *for you or against you*. If you decide it would be a constructive step to take then keep it brief and to the point. Thank the interviewer for seeing you. Say how you enjoyed the meeting which confirmed your view that the job on offer is well-suited to your abilities and experience. Say how you hope you will have the opportunity of working with the company and that you look forward to hearing the decision.

Chase the interviewer for a decision

At the end of your interview the interviewer should have given you a fairly accurate idea of the date by which a decision should be made. Note the date in your diary. If the day goes past and you have heard nothing telephone or write and ask for news. You have a right to know one way or the other.

Get constructive criticism from the interviewer

If you are rejected the most constructive thing you can do is to phone or write and ask for the reasons why. Explain that you are not querying the decision but that you would appreciate the information if at all possible, as you will then be able to learn from it for another occasion. This is a hard piece of follow-up advice, but if you can steel yourself to do it you will probably gain valuable insights into your interview performance and into which particular lack of experience or qualifications is holding you back.

Coping with rejection

An important part of interview follow-up is coping with possible rejection. Usually many more people apply for a job than can be successful. You should not take rejection too personally in these circumstances, but you should do all you can to build on the experience. The important thing is to approach each interview as a totally separate entity. *Do not* carry feelings of rejection from one situation over into the next. If you do you will approach the next interview in the wrong frame of mind and it will make you less effective.

Keep your options open

If you have not pinned all your hopes on one job you will be less vulnerable if you are turned down. Make a point of always having more than one project on the go. This will affect your interview, as subconsciously you will not be as desperate as someone who has directed all their energy and aspirations into one make-or-break situation. A 'desperate' candidate stands much less chance than a more relaxed candidate who goes into the interview knowing that she/he has other options. It will also help you if you are rejected as you will be too busy planning for the next project to allow yourself to come to a full stop. Never sit about waiting for the result of one interview. Start making more applications immediately.

Keep file and comments for reference

Keep your interview file together with your post-interview checklist and any comments you may have gleaned from the interviewer or Personnel Department through your follow-up call. You may be recalled for a second interview or apply to the same place some time in the future. Either way your interview file will make valuable background reading.

3

Variations on the Job Interview

Panel interviews

Sometimes you will be interviewed by several people together, in what is known as a panel interview. The panel will consist of a chairman and two or more additional people who are there because they have a particular area of expertise or responsibility. Panel interviews can be rather intimidating as it is easy to get a feeling of 'just me against all of them'. Good interviewers will try and prevent you from feeling overwhelmed but being outnumbered inevitably creates a certain tension.

Identify the most influential interviewer

In theory it is the chairperson, who sits in the middle, who is the most crucial member of the interview panel, but in practice one of the others may have the real power to make decisions or the personality to override the others. You should try and work out if any one person seems to carry more weight with the others and address your answers to that person whenever possible. Do not be fooled into thinking it is the noisiest or jokiest member of the panel. It is far more likely to be the person to whom the others seem to defer whenever there is any query or discussion.

Panel interviews, if they are well run and well organized, can be particularly searching. For the candidate the same basic rules of selling yourself apply as for one-to-one interviews. You should address your reply to whoever asked the actual question, try and include the person who seems most important in the general sweep of your glance and look to the chairman if there is any pause between questions.

Although panel interviews can seem intimidating, some of the questions you are most worried about may get forgotten because several people may be less well organized than one. In that case you will have fewer rather than more difficulties with which to cope.

Sequential interviews

A more demanding interview technique is the sequential interview. This means that you are seen by several people, individually, in succession, rather than facing them all as a group. For sequential interviews you need all your wits about you, which means being thoroughly well prepared and getting a decent night's sleep beforehand so your energy does not flag!

Group interviews

Group methods are used by large companies and organizations when dealing with applicants for jobs which require considerable organizational and leadership skills. The successful candidates will probably be given a very expensive training, and it is fear of wasting money on training unsuitable applicants which is the reason for such a prolonged exercise. Understanding your potential employer's motives may help you maintain your sense of humour throughout what can be a rather trying experience, not least because you are having to cooperate with your rivals and in some cases even help them out.

Clearly different employers will be looking for different things in group interviews. Try and understand what it is they are looking for. Stay alert and think on your feet.

Keep general knowledge up to date

It is always wise before any interview to make an effort to keep up with current affairs and to formulate reasoned opinions on some of the major issues. This is particularly important for group interviews where group discussion and the ability to reason through your own point of view and persuade others to your opinion are invariably a major feature. Lack of awareness of the world around you, and a mind which has no ideas of its own, will show up to greater disadvantage in direct comparison with your fellow interviewees than they will in a one-to-one interview.

Do not show off

Whether the day follows a pattern of group discussion alone or involves an element of competitiveness by dividing the overall group into smaller groups with set targets to achieve, you should bear in mind a few good rules. Be conscious of the difference between showing leadership qualities and simply showing off. You want to stand out in the assessor's mind but not as an insensitive bully trying to throw your weight around. A polite and considered approach, avoiding outright confrontation, will stand you in better stead.

Show you can work as part of a team

You will make a better impression if you shine by your own merits rather than trying to show how dull everyone else is. This is particularly true if you have been divided up into teams. Assessors will be looking to see how you cooperate with others and whether or not you can put the overall benefit of your own side before individual glory.

Have faith in the interviewers' experience

You will need to have confidence in those who are running the group interview. They are usually highly experienced in what they are doing and are unlikely to miss the truth of what is going on. So do not feel you have to make a fuss to get attention. If you feel confident in the assessors you can relax and behave as you should instead of feeling the need to get yourself noticed.

Do not deliberately keep a low profile

The same principle applies to those whose natural instinct is to try and merge with the wallpaper. It will do you no good to try and keep away from the hub of activity and hope that by making no impression you will not make a bad impression. A seasoned assessor will soon spot someone who is not taking an active and full part in the activity and it will be regarded as no better than trying to force your way on to the centre stage.

Accept responsibility

If you find yourself as a group leader or chairman accept the responsibility. Do not use the opportunity to throw your weight about but to enable your own group to handle whatever task or problem they have been allotted in the most efficient manner. Always stay calm and do not allow others to drag you in to a conflict of personalities. Once you have accepted responsibility do not allow someone else to take it away from you as that will be clear proof of your inability to handle the situation. Make sure everyone has a chance to have their say but be prepared to use your judgement when it comes to deciding when action should be taken.

Do not put on an act

Whatever happens do not try to be someone you are not. By all means work to emphasize your positive qualities and to control your weak points, but if you put on an act you are almost bound to get caught out and you certainly will not be able to relax.

Social interviews

Most interviews are rather formal situations where emphasis is placed on trying to create a relaxed atmosphere in an artificial situation. Social interviews, sometimes known as 'trial by sherry', are theoretically relaxed occasions, like a drinks party or dinner, but the atmosphere tends to become rather strained as one half of the party sizes up and assesses the other half.

Social interviews can vary from a candidate being taken over to the pub for a drink and a sandwich, so that future colleagues can see whether or not the newcomer will fit in, to full-scale formal affairs. Often it is the company wife who is being quietly summed up to see if she can 'keep up' with her husband or pull her weight in a job which makes a lot of social demands. Candidates who are involved in group interviews, which often stretch over one or two days, will also find themselves eating and socializing with their fellow candidates and assessors. Although these social situations are not strictly part of the scheduled group interview, candidates should always be aware that any awkwardness or irregularity in their behaviour will be noted. There are no temporary truces.

Be aware that you are being interviewed

Social interviews create several possible dangers. One is that those who are being assessed, however informally, will be blissfully unaware of what is going on and reveal far more about themselves than is wise.

Do not drink too much alcohol

If too much alcohol is consumed—and this is easily done—you may reveal a side of your nature which is not the real you. In any social situation connected with work, even if you are unaware of any assessment taking place, it is only common sense to limit your intake of alcohol. This is essential if you know it affects you badly. Unfortunately even today, when people are more aware of the dangers of too much alcohol, it is often socially unacceptable to seem to refuse the convivial offer of a drink. Men in particular may find this is a problem when the idea still persists that being able to hold your alcohol proves what a great guy you are.

However, do not make an issue of refusing a drink. Accept one and make it last as long as possible. At a meal have a glass of water as well as wine and keep sipping at the water so that it is not your wine glass which is being constantly refilled. Try drinking white wine mixed with sparkling mineral water or soda. After the initial whisky or gin and tonic move on to plain ginger ale or tonic water with ice and lemon which will give the impression, if necessary, that you are still drinking the real thing.

Try to act naturally

Another way of creating a bad impression at a social interview is by being so self-conscious and aware of what is going on that you are unable to act naturally and show yourself in the best possible light. If you feel very inhibited by the artificiality of the situation you will give a very inaccurate impression of the sort of person you really are, perhaps even overcompensating for nerves by being too gregarious and obvious and making it clear that you are not good at handling yourself in a social situation.

Treat a social interview seriously

The most important element in coping with a social interview well is coming to terms with the fact that it really is an interview. It is therefore not going to be possible to behave as though you were at a genuine social occasion and it will not be surprising if you feel awkward and nervous. Once you realize this you can start treating it like any other interview, and apply the same ground rules. Be punctual, pay attention to what you wear, be aware of how others are reacting to the signals you are sending out. Calm your nerves by deep breathing, not by having a stiff drink. Above all remember that you are selling yourself, so present yourself in a confident fashion but without boasting.

Demonstrate support for a partner

Spouses who know that the way they behave will affect their partners' chances of getting a job should try and find out beforehand what is expected of them. Being primed with the relevant background information can make you much more confident that you are saying the right thing to the right person. Above all try and make it clear that you are enthusiastic about the future project. If there are possible problems and conditions that make the company worried about how a partner will cope make it clear that you know what they are and that they are not problems to you. Obvious examples are travelling or living abroad, the husband having to be away for long periods, having to relocate, changing children's schools at an awkward stage in their career, having to do a lot of company entertaining. A cheerful and supportive disposition is what you are being assessed for. If you do have doubts and problems about the job these should be discussed privately before things reach a crucial stage. Do not use a social setting for suddenly coming out with all the reservations you may have or the frustrations you may feel at not having been consulted properly. Few things can be more guaranteed to create a negative response than the sight of husband and wife sparring in public.

Employment agencies

Employment agencies used to be only for domestic and office staff. Nowadays there is a large sector which deals with far more high-powered recruitment, and men are as likely as women to find themselves seeking work through an agency.

All the general advice given to improve your interview performance holds equally good when being interviewed by an agency and you can expect many of the same questions. However, at an agency you are more likely to be tested on your particular skills such as shorthand, typing, operating a VDU.

Appearance is important. Just because there is no job immediately on the horizon do not turn up looking a mess. The agency will be assessing you just as one of its clients will do. Many companies that recruit through agencies are particularly concerned with their company image and will be looking for staff who know how to dress appropriately. If you are not disciplined enough to arrive at the agency as though dressed for work you may not be taken on to the books.

First impressions are crucial. As well as being appropriately dressed you should also be aware that you may have been noted even while looking at the agency's window display. In a small employment agency there may only be one interviewer and you will put yourself at a disadvantage if you make a bad start. So, be presentable, be articulate and be pleasant to everyone you meet.

Have some ideas of your own

Have some idea before you go into an agency of what you want to do or the type of company for which you want to work. Clearly agencies dealing with executive appointments will have more time for discussion and advice about career moves and development than agencies dealing with general office staff. Even so you will gain more out of the interview if you have some clear ideas of your own about what you want to do, and also about what you do not want to do.

Take your c.v. with you

Take a comprehensive career history with you. This will save time and will be a clear indication that you are well organized. A good agency interviewer will look through it and pick up on the same gaps and discrepancies which will appear to the job interviewer but will not be looking with any one particular job in mind.

Do not be surprised if an agency interviewer is rather alarmingly direct. He or she is trying to get a very clear picture of what you can do so that they can place you accurately and not send you on too many pointless interviews. In effect they will be assessing you in much the same way that you make your own self-assessment and then trying to match you to jobs in the way that you should do when applying for jobs directly. You will get more out of the agency and interviewer and make their task easier if you have already made your own attempt at self-assessment (see p. 9).

The agency interviewer will be looking to see how you handle yourself during the interview. You should therefore make as much effort as you would if you were being interviewed for a particular job. Try to be relaxed, confident, pleasantly enthusiastic, and sell yourself without bragging. Make the most of any advice which you can get from the interviewer and follow up suggestions for improving your presentation and qualifications.

Occasionally agency interviewers may adopt a jaded and cynical approach, the result of seeing people day after day and forgetting that each one is an individual who should be assessed individually. If this is the case you may be better advised to find another agency. Do not allow yourself to be pushed around by an agency that tells you they have a large number of suitable vacancies and then persists in sending you for jobs which are not within your specifications.

PART II

Employment Interviews—
The Interviewer

Introduction:
What Makes a Good Interviewer?

The costs of poor interviewing

The purpose of the employment interview is to select the right person for the job. Failure to do so is expensive, in financial and human terms. Inability to select the right people is considered to be one of the major weaknesses of British management, a weakness with a hidden cost of many millions of pounds a year.

Employing the wrong people will be a waste of your and/or your company's time and assets, and will put pressure on existing staff who may have to work with unsatisfactory newcomers. It will also be unfair to the new employees. They will be put under the strain of doing jobs for which they are unsuited and as a result will either leave after a short time, have the humiliation of being told they are unsuitable, or cause difficulties for other staff who have to rely on them or cooperate with them.

Now that employment is hedged about with legislation a company may have difficulties and expense in shedding unsuitable workers.

Poor selection is largely the result of poor interviewing techniques. Staff is selected by hunches and instinct rather than a thorough assessment of candidates' abilities and qualities by an interviewer with a clear picture of the job which is to be filled.

A bad interviewer can give a potentially excellent employee such a negative impression that he or she loses interest in the job. This is a particular danger where candidates are being interviewed for high-ranking appointments, when incompetent interviewing may create a hostile reaction in the candidate who is being wooed.

Interviewing skills must be learned

Good interviewers are made, not born. That is not to say that some people are not naturally more perceptive, sympathetic and shrewd than others. But even if you have all the gifts essential for making a first-rate interviewer you will still benefit from learning as much as possible about the theory of interviewing and from practising your skills. Acquiring a good interview technique is as important for people employing one person to work directly for them as it is for those who will be taking on large numbers to work for a company.

The keys to good interviewing in all cases are thorough preparation, knowing exactly what you are looking for and having confidence in your own judgement.

The methods and ideas given below should not necessarily be followed exactly. They should be regarded as basic guidelines and adapted to the many possible variables, such as type of employment, level of responsibility, age/experience of the candidates. Some of the procedures will only be used where quite large numbers are being interviewed, but the principle of thorough preparation is always the same.

4

Before the Interview

Who will be doing the interviewing?

At first sight this may seem an unnecessary question. There may either be a personnel officer who interviews all staff for a fairly large company, or there may be one person who will be so closely involved with the new employee that she/he seems the inevitable person to carry out the interview. However, things are rarely that simple. Even a woman wanting to take on help with child-care may have to consider whether or not she will make the decision herself or whether her husband or even the child itself will become involved. What needs to be discussed and understood is who is in the best position to make the final decision.

The two important, and possibly conflicting elements to be borne in mind are, who knows most about what the job involves and who is most skilled at the process of selection interviewing. If the answer cannot be given in the shape of one person then it may be better to hold panel or sequential interviews (see pp. 109–12). If the person who does the interviewing is not the person for whom the new employee will be working then it is essential that that person should at least be allowed to sit in on interviews and have an agreed say in the final decision. It is only sensible that the person for whom the candidate will be working (and who therefore probably knows best what is needed), should be involved in the selection. Conversely, it is reassuring to candidates to know, if they are successful, that they are there with the positive approval of the person for whom they are working.

Defining the job

It stands to reason that you cannot find the right person to do a job unless you know yourself exactly what that job is.

Write a clear job specification

It is essential that a really comprehensive and readily understood job description/specification is drawn up so that:

(a) the interviewer knows exactly what role the candidate will have to fulfil;

(b) the right type of candidate will recognize themselves when the job is advertised.

Even if you are a very small business or taking on domestic staff you should write a job specification, although you may prefer to make it a more informal list of everything the job entails.

Consult others

This means discussing the position, the work involved, the skills required, the type of personality who will fit in, with all the people who will expect to benefit from the new employee and then drawing up a written job description. If the person doing the interviewing is not the person for whom the candidate will be working directly that person's views should definitely be consulted.

Find the candidate for the job, not vice versa

If the job is a newly created one then clear guidelines should be drawn up of what the candidate will be expected to do, what qualifications, skills, abilities and personal qualities they will need. (Do not simply find a candidate you like then mould the job specification round his or her particular strengths.)

If the job already exists a job specification should still be drawn up as though the job were being created from scratch. The outgoing person who has been doing the job should be consulted as part of this, although it should be borne in mind that he or she may have certain prejudices which preclude their giving a totally satisfactory answer.

Identify and tackle any problems in the job

If you are replacing someone who is leaving the firm then it is essential to know why they are going. It may be for a perfectly simple reason, for example a partner may have found a job which entails moving out of the area. However, it may be because of some problem to do with the job itself or the working conditions. If there is a problem with the job then, if the criticism is valid, take this into account while working out the new job specification. Otherwise you may find the next person leaves as well and you will be involved with costly and time-consuming interview procedures again.

For the same reason, as well as in the interests of having contented employees, it is worth coming to grips with any difficulties in the work environment, such as conflicting personalities, before taking on a replacement.

Becoming an adept interviewer is an invaluable skill. However, unless you are a professional personnel officer, one of the proofs of your success will be in the fact that you do not have to exercise your interviewing skill too often, because you consistently choose the right people for the right jobs and they are therefore happy to stay.

Rethinking an existing job

Even if the outgoing employee has no constructive criticism to make of the job, the period of compiling the job specification prior to the interview is an invaluable chance to reconsider what exactly the job involves and to compare what is being done to what is really needed. This is especially valuable where a job has been done for a long time by the same person. That person may bring to it their own considerable skills and preferences but may have become inflexible and may have defined the job by their own way of doing it. Writing out a fresh job specification enables you to see the job objectively, possibly rethinking it to fulfil a more useful function. The new employee does not have to be an exact replacement of the former employee, but may be able to perform a more productive and better defined role.

Is there really a job there?

It is always possible that when you do the job specification of a long-standing job you will decide the job does not really need to exist at all! In many respects it may no longer fulfil a useful function and those parts of the job that are still useful could be distributed among existing staff. You may then decide that either you do not need to interview anyone at all because no job exists or that you need to interview someone for a quite different role, perhaps involving taking on various responsibilities of other employees which together form a more rational and cohesive whole.

Drawing up a personnel specification

Picturing the ideal candidate

Once you have an exact description of the job then you can move on to an accurate description of the ideal candidate to do it. This is sometimes known as a personnel specification and is an essential part of pre-interview preparation. You should never go into an interview without a very clear idea of the person you think would suit the post ideally. You should not find yourself saying, 'I don't know what I want but I think I'll recognize it when I see it'.

Method: separate essential and desirable qualities. A personnel specification is far easier to draw up than it sounds. The simplest way is to make three columns, one headed 'categories', the next headed 'essentials', and the third headed 'desirable'. In the first list your categories will cover the following topics: physical, qualifications, skills, experience, personality, personal circumstances, negative points. After careful consideration, after discussion with those who will be closely affected by your final decision, and adhering firmly to the job specification already drawn up, list your requirements under the appropriate heading. Pay particular attention to what is regarded as essential as these points should remain uppermost in your mind while making a preliminary selection from application forms and while interviewing. Listing the remaining requirements as merely 'desirable' will give you the flexibility you must still retain even in a well-planned interview. Of course any candidate specification, like any job description, should take account of legislation concerning race relations and equal opportunities for men and women. A typical ideal personnel specification might look like the table on the opposite page.

*   *   *

Job: Commissioning editor, children's books. Able to see project through to camera-ready artwork. Some writing involved. Further training in book production will be given if necessary.

Categories	Essential	Desirable
Qualifications	A levels or degree	English to A level Degree in English
Skills	Copy-editing Typing Making a paste-up Writing good simple English	Word processing Good general knowledge Familiar with technical side of book production
Experience	2 years minimum in publishing Some writing as part of work	Work in children's publishing Commissioning manuscripts Overseeing budgets
Physical	Able to manage office stairs	—
Personality	Able to work without supervision Calm under stress Flexible Gets on well with others	Ready to contribute own ideas Sense of humour Good telephone manner
Personal circumstances	Occasionally able to work late or over weekends	Able to start immediately Easy travel to work
Negative points	Must not smoke	—

Attracting the right applicants

When you know what the job is and what sort of person you would like to employ your next step is to look in the ideal place for applicants of the right calibre. The importance of this is often underestimated but it is essential that not only do you get applicants but applicants who genuinely fulfil your requirements. If not, your entire beautifully prepared interview may prove a waste of time and you run the risk of appointing someone who is the least unsuitable candidate rather than someone who satisfies all the specifications.

Agencies

One way of finding applicants of a suitable calibre is to use an agency which specializes in the type of employee you are looking for, and which, if it is a good agency, will already have done some preliminary sorting to weed out those who are entirely unsuitable. Agencies range from job centres to 'headhunters' who deal with what is often the very discreet transfer of high-powered executive personnel from one firm to another. Nowadays there are agencies to service most industries and professions, and of course there are agencies for office and domestic staff.

Use other methods in addition to agencies

However, although agencies take a lot of the work out of finding an employee, and can be particularly useful if interviewer(s) are part of a voluntary committee which has limited time to devote to the task of appointing new staff, they have the disadvantage that you are limited in your choice by the number of people who have themselves registered with the agency. If you do not advertise more widely your vacancy will not come to the attention of other potential employees who may not be actively looking for a job but who might be attracted by an advertisement which clearly specifies someone like them. It is probably better to use an agency in addition to the other methods available.

Let existing staff apply

If you are not going to confine your search to the agencies then you must consider very carefully what your options are. The first option, where relevant, is to let other employees in your organization know that a vacancy exists. Only do this where you think there may actually be someone of the right calibre available. It is unfair on the candidates to raise their hopes unnecessarily, and is a waste of your own time.

Newspaper and trade journals

Another alternative is to advertise in newspapers and trade journals. You will probably know which ones are read by the type of staff you have in mind.

Advertising agencies

If you are going to spend a lot of money advertising nationally, or if you are very inexperienced, you might like to enlist the help of an advertising agency. A reputable agency will advise you on the wording and placing of your advertisement and may even take its fee from the newspaper not from the client.

Make advertisements accurate and informative

Advertising should be based on the accurate job description you have already drawn up, so that the right sort of people will recognize themselves. Advertising should also include those features which will prove attractive to candidates, such as salary, working conditions, promotion prospects, benefits, etc.

Make the advertisement clear and honest. One of the most important rules of interviewing is to give candidates a clear understanding of what the job entails. If this is not done a disillusioned employee may well leave after a short time and you will have to repeat the expensive and disruptive process of interviewing all over again. Although an advertisement is not the place in which to list all the snags of the job it should mention fundamental conditions like shift work or weekend working so you do not waste time seeing people for whom such conditions would be unacceptable.

Word-of-mouth advertising

Lastly, just as people looking for jobs are advised to ask around and find out about prospects through the grapevine rather than from official sources, employers too, where appropriate, can let it be known that they are looking for a certain sort of employee.

Take advice, and use whatever method you think will be most effective in attracting the right sort of people along for interview, so that you will be making a selection from a number of genuinely suitable candidates.

Giving the company a good name

Always acknowledge all replies you receive from advertisements. This is not only a matter of common courtesy but will help create/ maintain your image as a good employer. In the long term treating your staff and potential staff well will increase your chances of attracting high-calibre applicants for job vacancies.

Application Forms

Using application forms

Application forms are not just a routine procedure. They fulfil a very necessary two-fold function. They are documents of record, and they provide basic information for an initial selection or 'interview'. In this book we are dealing with the second function; application forms as a means of making an initial selection. Use them intelligently by asking the right questions on the form, interpreting the answers correctly and comparing the candidates' qualifications to the job and personnel specifications you have drawn up. You can then eliminate all but the genuinely suitable applicants without having to interview an enormous number of people in person.

When application forms are not necessary

You will not need to use application forms if you are employing people where skill in reading and writing are not important. If you want their details for records then it is simpler to fill in the form yourself while conducting the interview rather than submit the candidates to the unnecessary stress of coping with a form. Equally you will not need an application form, except possibly for the record, if you are seeing a single applicant who has applied for the job 'on spec.' Private/domestic employers will not usually need to use application forms, although they should use letters of application to make a preliminary comparison and selection of candidates, rather as though they were using application forms.

Using standard forms

Because application forms provide the basis of what is in reality a preliminary round of the interview they should be well thought out. Questions should be formulated with a definite purpose and not just asked as a matter of course. It is possible to buy well-designed general purpose application forms (details are given at the back of the book). These are adequate for most purposes if they are used properly, since different people will be able to deduce from the answers information which is relevant to the job they want to fill.

Designing your own forms

If you have very specific qualifications and abilities in mind then you may need to devise an application form of your own. If you do, remember to keep it simple and straightforward. It is better to manage without sections for office use, which candidates may find confusing and alienating. Always leave plenty of space for answers—some forms seem devised to eliminate anyone with normal or large handwriting.

Below are some points which you may wish to include in your application form. You should add your own questions to ascertain the candidate's technical knowledge and expertise in the field in which you are dealing.

Personal details Name, address, telephone number, date of birth, marital status, number of children, state of health, height/weight.

Job application Name of job, where seen advertised, date available to start, any previous applications to the same company.

Education Schools attended and dates, examinations passed and dates, examinations tried unsuccessfully and dates, any awards/ prizes, extracurricular activities, any responsibilities. University/college attended and dates, course taken, examinations passed and grades, awards/prizes, extracurricular activities, any responsibilities.

Training Type of training (college, part-time, night school, etc.), courses taken (including apprenticeships, articles, etc.), professional qualifications achieved and dates, membership of professional bodies (if so, which level), additional skills/training, for example, foreign languages, specific machinery.

Family background Occupations of parents and brothers and sisters, any relatives employed in the same trade/profession, any relatives employed by the same company.

Work history Chronological record of employment, details of work involved and areas of responsibility, reasons for leaving, current employment, current salary, reasons for leaving present job.

Leisure interests: Hobbies, membership of organizations, travel, etc.

General information Major areas of interest at work and leisure, self-assessment of strengths and weaknesses, ambitions.

Technical questions/specific requirements (Detailed questions relevant to the requirements of the job.)

Photograph (A passport-size photograph can be extremely useful if you have a number of people to interview. It will literally put a face to a name and be a useful memory aid when you compare notes and come to a final decision after the interviews.)

Application forms are preferable to c.v.s

Of course you can make a preliminary selection using c.v.s compiled by the applicants themselves, but this allows candidates to present information in a way which suits them. *A standardized application form makes direct comparisons much easier.*

Sending out application forms

When applicants respond to an advertisement they should be sent an application form to fill in unless the initial letter was so poor that it warrants an immediate rejection.

If a letter is very good and the applicant clearly fits the job/personnel specification fairly well you may wish to send out an appointment for an interview at the same time as the application form.

In the majority of cases you will simply send the application form and use the completed forms as the means of eliminating the applicants who are clearly unsuitable.

To make these decisions you will have to do very much what you will be doing during the interview itself. That is, going through various categories—education, qualifications, experience, etc., and seeing how they match up with the picture of the ideal candidate which you built up. In some sense it will be more difficult because you will not be able to ask for further details. On the other hand you will be able to be much more objective and not allow yourself to be unduly influenced by personality when the fundamental qualifications and expertise are missing.

If the essential educational standard or technical skills required by the job/personnel specification are not there then the candidate can be quickly rejected. It would be a waste of time for both of you to go on to an interview. Answers about personal qualities and abilities are harder to interpret, although experience does make it easier. Do not be surprised if you reject as many as 50 per cent of the candidates at this stage.

If you are in two minds then give the candidate the benefit of the doubt and allow him or her to come for interview and elaborate on the details given on the form. Although application forms can be very thorough and very revealing there are some questions which can only be asked face to face, and in an interview where a good rapport has been established. For example, people may be under-standably reluctant to commit their personal financial details to paper, or discuss the real reasons why they may have left one of their previous jobs.

Using the application form to plan the interview

Application forms (or c.v.s if application forms are not available) should be used as the basis for the candidate's interview. This will be a far easier task if the initial advertisement/job description has been accurate enough to attract people with the right qualifications and experience. These candidates will then have been able to gauge their answers to give information which is closely relevant to the job.

You should structure your interview round the information you have been given and not waste time asking again what you already know from the form. Pay particular attention to any areas which may be problematic—unexplained gaps in work sequence, poor examination results, etc. Notes of questions arising out of the application form should be attached to it and used as a memory aid during the interview.

Further information on structuring the interview is given on p. 94 in Chapter 5.

Take up references

Once you have decided to see an applicant, any references given in the application form (or c.v.), including telephone references, should be taken up *before* the interview.

Arranging the interview

Arranging the interview in an organized fashion, and making sure it takes place in relaxing circumstances, are very important if you are to see the candidates at their best and so be able to make a well-informed decision.

If you are delegating any of the responsibility for these arrangements be sure to make a list so no one is in any doubt about their particular tasks and you can check they have been done.

Making an interview schedule

The first thing is for the interviewer to find a time and date which are suitable. Of course as the interviewer you basically arrange the interview to suit yourself. You are the person who has the initiative, so you should never need to arrange interviews, even one-off interviews, when you are pressed for time. Having to check your watch will have a bad effect on the way you handle the interview and what you learn from it.

It is also up to you to allot time for the interviews so that you can send candidates accurate appointments. Thirty minutes is usually sufficient for an interview, but allow an hour or even more if the appointment is a high-powered one and the interview will be very searching. You may also need slightly longer for a panel interview.

Leave enough time between interviews

When calculating appointment times bear in mind that you will need five full minutes minimum before and after each interview (ten minutes between interviews). The first five minutes is to enable you to reflect on the candidate who has left and to jot down any opinions and comments which are fresh in your mind. You will then need a further five minutes to look through the application form (or application letter or c.v.) of the next candidate, and to remind yourself of any particular questions which need to be asked as a result of what it contained. Never go straight on from one candidate to the next without pause for reflection, no matter how rushed you feel. If you do, you will find it almost impossible to differentiate one candidate from another by the end of the day and you will run a very high risk of making a bad decision.

Take a 'tour' into account

Another point to bear in mind when working out your interview schedule is whether or not candidates are to be shown over the work place before the interview. If so, estimate how long this will take, call the candidates for interview that much earlier than you would otherwise have done, and let them know in the letter that they are to be given a tour first.

If you are going to show candidates around then make sure there is someone to do it and that anyone whose work/routine might be affected has been given some advance warning. If you will want the reactions of these people to the candidate be sure to let them know that this will be expected.

Consider the possibility of 'out-of-hours' interviewing

It may not always be possible, but consider the feasibility of holding some of the interviews at weekends or in the evenings. It is often extremely awkward for people to take time off work, and it is probably the very people who would be most reluctant to lie or make excuses for their absence to their present employers who will be the best candidates from your point of view.

Keep waiting to a minimum

You should also take the candidate into account by arranging appointments so that waiting time is kept to a minimum.

Inform everyone who may be involved

Other people apart from yourself and the candidate who may need to be taken into account when fixing a schedule are:

(a) fellow interviewers if this is to be a panel or sequential interview;
(b) members of staff who may be required to brief candidates or show them around;
(c) anyone higher up the scale who likes to oversee any possible appointments.

You should also make sure that the person who will be acting as receptionist is properly briefed. If relevant, inform any peripheral staff such as gate-keepers who will need names, or tea ladies who may need extra supplies.

If you are going to pay candidates' travelling expenses one of the advance preparations will be to organize these beforehand, ensuring there is cash available or that someone will be there to sign the necessary cheque.

Put appointments in writing

Candidates should always be informed in writing about their appointments. If possible have an alternative date available and give them the option of telephoning to change their original appointment. This may not be feasible where there is a very large number of candidates, but if people have got through the original application forms stage of selection it will be worth making an effort to see them in person. If revised arrangements are made over the telephone, these, too, should be confirmed in writing.

Confirm telephone appointments

When initial appointments are made over the telephone, for

instance if someone telephones to ask about vacancies, these should also be confirmed in writing.

If you yourself have to alter an arrangement try to give as much warning as possible. This will be appreciated by the candidate and prevent any unnecessary bad feeling that would affect the outcome.

Send travel details

When writing you may like to include a simple map and travel details to help candidates arrive on time.

Ensure a relaxed environment

Proper attention should be given to ensuring that the conditions for the interview are as relaxed as possible. There should be a proper waiting room, with chairs, magazines to read and cloakroom facilities easily accessible. Even if this is difficult to provide, candidates should not have to wait around in a very public area. It is unnecessarily unnerving to be waiting your turn while potential workmates eye you up and down.

Ensure that candidates are expected and greeted

You should also arrange for someone to act as a receptionist. This is essential if quite large numbers of candidates will be coming during the day as they will need to be organized and someone will have to handle any unforeseen changes in schedule. Even if you are only seeing a few people there should be someone to greet them on arrival and make them feel they have come to the right place on the right day. If your organization is slap-happy it will unnerve candidates and may make them think twice before accepting a job with you.

Avoid noise and interruptions

The room used for the interview should be quiet and away from the general office traffic and bustle. If you are using your own office rather than an interview room, arrange for telephone calls to be intercepted and make sure you are not disturbed or distracted while interviewing.

If you need to book a special interview room in your own building or in an hotel make sure it is done well in advance and before you inform the candidates of the arrangements. Last-minute alterations do not encourage confidence in the interviewer.

Arranging the room layout

The room itself should be arranged to encourage the candidate to relax and talk freely. It should not always be necessary to stick to the traditional layout of interviewer behind a desk and candidate in a chair immediately in front, as if about to undergo an interrogation. Unless you want to intimidate the people you are seeing (and you will get a less truthful picture of them if you do) then consider conducting the interview in two fairly comfortable chairs placed at angles next to each other. A small table can be used for any notes, water, etc. If you think you will need to write during the interview then attach your notes to a clipboard. This informal arrangement may also help you to relax—interviewers get nervous too!

If you are conducting an interview in less formal surroundings, in your own home for instance, or in a workshop, the same principles apply. Try to find somewhere where the interviewee can feel reasonably relaxed and you yourself can feel confident. If you have no secretary to fend off telephone calls turn the telephone off or take it off the hook while you are conducting the interview. Do not try to hold an interview, however informal, while 'on the run'. Always find time to sit down and devote your entire attention to what you are doing.

5

Conducting the Interview

The form of the interview

The form of the interview should be seen in the context of its main objectives.

Objects of the interview

First and foremost you are looking to find the candidate who is most ideally suited to doing the job. This means not taking on someone who is too highly qualified and would be easily bored or dissatisfied as much as finding someone with the ability to do the job.

Second, you are looking for a candidate who will find that his or her own requirements are met by the conditions of the job and the organization (whether it be a large company or a one-to-one working relationship). If this is not the case, then an otherwise ideal candidate may turn out to be unhappy doing the work and therefore fundamentally unsuitable.

Third, you are aiming to create an atmosphere in the interview which will encourage the candidates to talk and show themselves to best advantage. You can then make the best informed decision and the candidates will feel that they have been fairly treated with ample opportunity to state their case.

Showing candidates around (optional). A short guided tour of the workplace, with explanations and a chance to ask questions may come first. This may well be done by someone other than the interviewer.

If not, you may like to give candidates a short written summary about the job, the company, pay and conditions, to read while they are waiting for interview. This can save a lot of time if there are many candidates who will all ask similar questions during the interview.

Look over the candidate's notes. Leave five minutes before each interview to look at the candidate's application form/letter, and any particular questions noted down while first reading it.

Initial greeting. Greet the interviewee as she/he comes in to the room. Confirm the candidate is the one you are expecting—you do not want any cases of mistaken identity. Allow a minute or two of informal chat to relax both of you. Some interviewers address candidates by their first names thinking it encourages a relaxed atmosphere. This is not a good idea as it puts the candidate in the awkward position of not knowing how to address *you*. Over-familiarity at this stage also makes asking awkward questions more difficult.

Smoking

When the candidate has settled ask him or her if they would like to smoke (if you yourself do not mind). A candidate should not smoke unless invited to do so. If you do not like smoking you should say so if the candidate asks, especially if that may prove a stumbling block in the future.

Be honest with the candidate

Bear in mind right from the start that the *interview is a two-way process*. On major and minor issues you should give fair answers to queries about the job to avoid misunderstandings and resentment later on. However good you become at assessing a candidate from your own point of view, you will have failed as an interviewer if you do not keep the second interview objective clearly in mind.

Tell the candidate about the interview and the job. Give the candidate a little more time to relax by filling him or her in on background information:

(a) who you are, the shape of the interview, how long it will take and what you are hoping to learn. This will not only reassure the candidate you know what you are doing, which will encourage his/her cooperation, it will also keep it clear in your own mind.

(b) about the job and the company.

Taking notes

If you are going to take notes, let the candidate know at this stage, explain that you do it for all the candidates, and that they are nothing sinister but simply a memory aid.

Because they distract the candidate, and you yourself may miss something important while noting a previous point, notetaking should be kept to a minimum during the interview. Try and keep the majority of writing to the period of five minutes or so after the interviewee has left, when you should sum up the points while they are fresh in your mind.

When you take notes during the interview it is a good idea to do so a short while after the relevant moment has passed so that the candidate is not aware of what prompted you to write. This way she/he will not be thrown by watching you note each unfortunate remark or be distracted by trying to work out what goes down well with you.

Questioning the candidate

The questions are the central point of the whole interview procedure and should be planned in advance. Knowing you have a structured interview to progress through will make you less likely to fall into the trap of making an intuitive decision at the opening stages of the interview.

You will not be able to find out all you need to know if you do not have a clear idea *before* you go into the interview of:

(a) what the job is;
(b) who the ideal candidate would be;
(c) what questions will enable you to discover whether the interviewee has all the necessary qualifications, abilities and qualities to match your mental picture of the ideal candidate.

Cover straightforward questions first. It is usual to cover the obvious questions about background, education, qualifications and experience first. These will be simpler for the candidate to answer and will therefore help to keep the atmosphere relaxed.

If application forms/c.v.s have been used correctly many of these questions will already have been answered and the well-prepared interviewer will have familiarized himself/herself with the details. In which case at this stage the interviewer can move quickly on to more detailed questions.

Candidates will be reassured if they find that the interviewer has taken the trouble to become familiar with the details on the form. This will make them readier to respond to supplementary questioning. Make it clear that you have taken in details by phrasing questions along the lines of, 'I've looked at your educational record which seems excellent but could you perhaps tell me why you did not pass maths until two years after your other O levels/changed schools halfway through A levels/took a year off while doing your degree?'

Any points similar to these which arise from any section of the application form/c.v. should be noted and taken in to the interview as a reminder.

When the more straightforward side of the questioning has been dealt with it is usual for the interviewer to move on to more difficult areas of assessment—motivation, enthusiasm, ability to fit in with existing staff, flexibility, readiness to travel if necessary, stability of home background, etc.

Prepare a list of questions to structure the interview. You cannot rely on the right questions coming to you on the spur of the moment. So a list of questions to winkle out the facts not covered by the application form or c.v. should be prepared before the interview.

Many books written for full-time or professional interviewers advocate a 'system' for asking questions. This usually involves grouping questions round a carefully devised plan, a five-point plan or a seven-point plan, designed to cover all aspects of a candidate's achievements and personality and weighing up excellence in one area such as 'motivation' against inadequacy in another such as 'background'. Although these methods are fairly simple, very thorough and no doubt excellent for those who make interviewing a large part of their life's work they are not particularly useful for those who may not need to exercise interviewing skills often but who want to use the interview to good effect when they do.

Simple method of comparison. Instead of trying to sort answers into meaningful groups it probably suits most people best if they use a percentage system. The principle of this is quite simple. Work out what you want to know, write down the approximate question you think will bring out the right answer and then in a third column put a percentage to represent how much the answer equates with what you would like to hear. Where there is a definite negative response put 0 per cent. If the candidate gives the one acceptable answer put 100 per cent. Other answers will be rated somewhere in between.

Begin with the questions that are obvious to you and using the same method move on to devise questions which will tell you more complex information about the candidate. When you are satisfied with your interview structure take a copy for each candidate and keep it with their application form and the additional questions which arose from it.

Below are some examples using this method. First a fairly simple question:

Topic	Question	Percentage
Foreign language	Do you have any knowledge of a foreign language?	60 per cent

The candidate's answer had been: 'I tried O level French but failed the oral exam'.

At the other end of the scale you might find:

Topic	Question	Percentage
Initiative	What would you do if a retailer telephoned to say an entire batch of skirts had been fitted with faulty zips?	90 per cent

The candidate's answer included apologizing, informing the sales manager immediately, checking remaining garments for faults, juggling orders to ensure a prompt replacement.

Topic	Question	Percentage
Flexibility	How would you feel if you had to work some evenings/weekends?	70 per cent

Candidate's answer: 'Of course I don't mind when things are very hectic, I'm always keen to pull my weight. However, our children are still very young and I think my wife would find it difficult if evening and weekend working became a regular commitment.'

Retain flexibility even in a planned interview. No two candidates will respond to questions in exactly the same way so you must keep a fair amount of flexibility in your approach—it would be wrong to stop a candidate from following up an interesting and potentially revealing answer simply because it is not coming at the designated point in your schedule. However, an inexperienced interviewer may find it difficult to get back on course again.

Guide candidates to relevant answers. A useful way of keeping candidates to the order which suits you, apart from giving them an idea of the sequence of questioning at the top of the interview, is to preface each group of questions with an explanatory sentence or two. For example, 'Thank you, I think that tells me all I need to know about your previous jobs. I should now like to take a look at your suitability for this particular job,' or 'If we could move on from your qualifications I'd like you to tell me a little more about your personal interests and hobbies'.

These rather artificial bridges from one group of questions to another are useful for keeping the candidate's mind focused on the right area of response and for helping the interviewer see his/her way through the prearranged structure of the interview. If a good rapport has been created with the candidate she/he will see it as further proof that you are in full command of what is happening in the interview and that all your questions are relevant.

Keep reminders on your question sheet. You may find it useful actually to write similar sentences or even your introductory chat on your question list to remind you if your mind goes a blank and to help you see the shape of the interview you are planning.

Keep awkward questions until later. If you have difficult or embarrassing questions to ask—about an unfavourable response to a reference, for example—leave it until the latter part of the interview when you have built up a reasonable rapport with the interviewee.

Use interview records to compare candidates. As long as you can stay reasonably flexible a well-planned interview structure will make comparisons between candidates much easier because all candidates will have been put through more or less the same hoops. The completed interview question forms together with answers to the individual questions arising from candidates' application forms/ c.v.s can be perused afterwards at comparative leisure. A decision can then be made on genuine grounds of comparative suitability, not just who sticks in the interviewer's mind most.

Some questions you may like to ask candidates

(If you did not use application forms or receive c.v.s then refer also to the basic list of questions, p. 100.)

Preliminary

- How was your journey?
- Do you live far?
- Have you always lived locally?

Talk about job/interview

- What do you know about us/the company?
- What general information have you about the job/interview?

Education/qualifications

- What did you enjoy most about school/college/any training?
- What did you dislike most about school/college/training?
- Why did you choose that particular course?
- Do you feel your training was useful for your job?
- How would you have changed it?
- What was your favourite subject at school/college. Why?
- What was your least favourite subject at school/college? Why?
- How would you describe your results?
- Have you done any further study/training since leaving school/ college?
- Do you study for enjoyment or to advance your career?

Personality

- Tell me something about yourself.
- How do you think your family background has influenced your working life?
- What interests do you have outside work?
- Have you ever been in a position of authority at school/college/in your social life?
- How do you feel about taking on responsibility?
- How do you get along with other people?
- What do you regard as your particular strengths?
- What do you regard as your particular weaknesses?
- How would you describe yourself to others?
- Which newspapers do you read?
- How would you like to see yourself in ten years' time?
- Have you discussed this job with your husband/wife?

Career

- What made you decide on X as a career/job?
- Are any of your family involved in similar work?

- Does it have any major drawbacks?
- Why have you had so many/few different jobs in the last few years?
- Where have you most enjoyed working?
- Why did you leave?
- What has been your most valuable working experience?
- What additional training have you had while working?
- Have you ever had to take time off for health reasons?
- Questions related to technical expertise.

The job itself

- Why are you looking for another job?
- What sort of a job do you want?
- What made you apply for this particular job?
- Why do you think you would be better than the other candidates?
- How do you think you will cope with the lack of . . . area of experience?
- How do you think your career to date has fitted you for this particular job?
- How will you cope with . . . drawbacks? (the long journey, moving house, children's schools, shift work, weekend work, long hours, frequent foreign travel, or any other drawbacks associated with the job)
- When would you be free to start?

Sweep-up questions

- What was your proudest moment?
- What was your worst moment?
- Who do you admire most/least?
- Is there anything else you'd like to tell me about yourself?

Let the candidate do most of the talking. Your aim should be to let the candidate do about 75 per cent of the talking. You will only find out what you need to know by really listening to what is said to you.

Ask supplementary questions. If candidates' responses do not tell you what you need to know then follow up your initial question with a more specific one. Do not allow yourself to be fobbed off without getting the information you need. Not all candidates are shrinking violets. Some may be strong characters or clever talkers. Your list of questions will be a considerable help in these cases as there will be obvious gaps to come back to if you have not been able to fill in a percentage answer.

Even when you get what you think is a good answer make sure it is substantiated. For example you may ask, 'How do you think you will manage working with a large number of school-leavers in the department?' The candidate may say there would be no problem. You could take their word for it and leave it at that. However, it would be far better to follow it up with a more specific question, 'Have you ever worked with that age group before?' If the candidate replies that she/he helped run a youth club in the town where she/he lived before you can be reasonably sure that a large number of young people is not going to come as a strange new experience.

A useful phrase to have on the tip of your tongue is, 'Why do you say/think that?'

Although you should be helpful and guide the candidate through the interview do not go too far and start 'pointing' him or her at the right answers.

Let the candidate ask questions

The question, 'Is there anything you would like to ask me' generally comes towards the end of the interview. It is a question which is relevant at all levels, from taking on a gardener to employing a managing director, but there is a tendency to treat it merely as a formality. However, the candidate's response can be very revealing and interviewers should pay attention to it.

For example, if you have already made available literature dealing with questions such as holidays/pensions/conditions of work and the candidate chooses to ask about them it may well indicate that she/he is the sort of person who does not do their background work thoroughly. The candidate whose immediate queries are along the lines of, 'When will I get my first pay rise?', or 'Will I be able to go on holiday in July?' will probably not be putting the job first and certainly lacks the good sense and tact to make it appear to be the priority.

Conversely, candidates whose questions show a high degree of motivation (asking about further training for example) and enthusiasm for the company and/or job will probably make the most satisfactory employees.

If there has genuinely been no opportunity for the candidate to find out about practical matters of pay and conditions in advance then it is sensible to discuss them at this stage, and you should have all the necessary details ready.

Although you should have a clear idea of how you would expect and like candidates to reply to this and other questions do bear in mind that nervousness can have an effect on what people say. It is an important part of your role as an interviewer to help the candidate relax enough to show himself or herself in as accurate and good a light as possible. However, some people are more affected by nerves than others so be ready to take this into account and to give people a chance to rethink or rephrase an answer, especially if it seems out of keeping with previous answers or what you know about them from their c.v./application form.

Although you should make a specific time when candidates can ask their own questions you should also allow time for questions which arise naturally at an earlier stage of the interview. If the interview goes well there should be a reasonable amount of give and take of information throughout.

Concluding the interview

When you have reached the end of your questions and/or the time allotted and the candidate has no further questions you must take the initiative to wind up the interview. There is no need to linger over this stage. Just use a simple phrase like, 'Well, I think you've told me all I need to know, thank you very much for coming to see us'. If the candidate seems settled in for the day stand up and help him/her with their coat, or begin to walk towards the door. At this stage you should explain what arrangements (if any) have been made for expenses.

Tell the candidate what is happening at the next stage in the selection and/or the date when you will be letting people know your decision.

Taking photographs. If dealing with a large number of candidates you may like to ask the candidate if you may take a polaroid picture for the application form if this has not been supplied already.

Show the candidate to the door and say goodbye while shaking hands so that the interview is properly rounded off and the candidate leaves with the impression of having been dealt with fairly and politely.

Asking the candidate to wait on for a few minutes. You may feel that as you make your notes immediately following the interview there will be points which you may like to clarify, particularly in a panel interview where different people may have formed different impressions. If you think this is the case then ask the interviewee to remain in the waiting room for five minutes in case you wish to ask them back. If this is the case do be sure to let the person know when they can leave.

Immediate post-interview assessment

As soon as the candidate has left the room make notes of your impressions of various abilities, making sure you have covered all the points used for the job/personnel specification, or the list of essential qualities and qualifications which you have drawn up if you are interviewing on a less formal basis. It is essential to do this while the interview is still fresh in your mind and before you see someone else who will inevitably erase what you remember of the previous applicant. If you are using a question sheet with space for percentage judgements on various topics make sure you have filled it in so that you can later compare candidates on all the headings.

At this stage make a note of any necessary further action such as recalling the candidate for a second interview, or following up references.

Reaching a decision

This is the whole point of the interview. *Do not rush into a decision.* When you have finished your interviews you should leave yourself time, not necessarily on the same day, to make an unhurried and carefully considered decision. Try not to be rushed into a decision and particularly do not offer a job immediately at the time of the interview or commit yourself before you have seen all the candidates, even if you are very sure that you have seen the right person for the job.

First of all you should eliminate all those who do not have the essential qualifications for the job you listed while you were still being objective and were not influenced by the different personalities of the candidate.

Factors which may unduly influence your judgement

You may be one of those people who is easily swayed by a

superficially attractive candidate with a strong personality, or you may be someone who is most influenced by the person you last spoke to.

You may be someone who has acknowledged biases and prejudices which are hard to set aside when making decisions, but which might lead you to overlook a suitable candidate if you did not use the job and personnel specifications as your guideline.

Another familiar failing of which you should be aware is the subconscious tendency of some interviewers to always look for someone who is like them and therefore to judge people on how far they match up. Try and be aware of this as a problem, asking yourself whether the candidate is genuinely not suitable but simply someone who does not fit in with your own picture of yourself. This is one problem of interviewing which is better handled by panel interviews than the one-to-one variety.

At the same time the question of personality is important and the most ideal candidate on paper may be unsuitable because his or her personality would make it difficult to work comfortably with the rest of the staff.

Imagine each of the candidates actually doing the job and dealing with the problems which might arise.

Emphasize the key factors

If you have to make a close-run decision then ask yourself which factor is the most important one and which candidate made the best showing on that particular subject.

Choose the most suitable candidate, not just the most highly qualified

Do not necessarily give the job to the most highly qualified candidate. You are looking for someone who is ideally suited to the vacancy and who will be happy to stay. You may find that an over-qualified person will quickly become dissatisfied and leave.

Do you really want the best of a bad bunch?

If none of the candidates is suitable or fulfils the basic requirements of the job/personnel description think twice before appointing the best of a bad bunch. You may be better advised to start again, possibly finding your candidates by a different method, than risk the problems of engaging an inadequate candidate and being faced with all the disruption of having to go through the whole process at a later stage anyway.

In the final analysis you will have to make a decision that should be based on the most objective assessment you can make but relying to a certain extent on your own instinct and intuition.

Informing successful candidates

When you have reached your decision let the chosen candidate know in writing. If you work for a fairly large company you probably have a standard procedure for informing new employees about conditions of work, etc. If you are new to the interviewing business then you must be sure to let the new employee have clear information about starting date, hours, holiday dates and any other conditions of work.

Informing unsuccessful candidates

When your offer has been accepted you should send out letters to the unsuccessful candidates. Make these letters as friendly as possible. If you were particularly impressed by any of the candidates you may like to say that you have retained details on file in case anything suitable should turn up in the future. Apart from the fact that polite letters of rejection are a matter of common courtesy there is also the more pragmatic point that something may go wrong with the new arrangement—the employee may change his/her mind, become ill, move away unexpectedly, take up another job at the last minute. It will be much easier to reactivate the application of an unsuccessful candidate who has been let down gently.

Interview follow-up

With each interview you gain more experience and expertise. To gain the maximum benefit from each interview (if you are aiming to learn a proper selection technique rather than treat each interview selection as a one-off event) you should do a thorough follow-up. This means keeping all the paperwork relevant to the successful candidate, including the job/personnel specifications, the advertisement used and most especially the notes you yourself made during the interview, immediately afterward and while making the final selection. Use your notes to compile a summary of the candidate and why you selected him/her for the job.

After six months, when the new employee has had a chance to settle in and learn the ropes, make a thorough and honest assessment of how well she/he is fulfilling the requirements. If you yourself are not directly involved consult those people who are working closely with the person. Compare your new assessment with your summary at the time of the interview. The more successful the new employee is being, the more successful you can assume your interview technique has been.

If the appointment is not wholly satisfactory, look at your notes and try and see where you made your mistakes. Think about how you could have foreseen them. Have you fallen into any obvious traps: failing to make a proper specification of the job requirements in the first place; not having a really clear picture of the ideal candidate in your mind; being swayed by an attractive and forceful personality; doing more talking than listening; looking for people with your own characteristics; appointing someone who lacks some of the points you had decided were essential; choosing the best of the bunch instead of rethinking; rushing the interviews in circumstances which do not allow a proper conversation? If you have ended up with an unsatisfactory employee the chances are there was a flaw in your selection procedure. The six-month assessment will at least allow you to learn from your mistakes by pinpointing which of the pitfalls mentioned during this section you may have fallen into. The next time you will be much more on your guard to avoid the same interviewing fault.

Summary

Good interviewers:

- work out exactly what the job entails;
- have a clear picture of the person they are looking for;
- work out the qualifications and experience which that person should have;
- attract candidates of the right calibre by wording job specifications correctly and advertising in the right places;
- absorb details on the candidate's application form and c.v. prior to the interview;
- prepare in advance a set of questions to investigate very thoroughly if the candidate has the expertise and personality necessary for the job;
- ask questions in a logical sequence;
- avoid woolly, general questions;
- do not run out of questions;

- put the candidate at ease, are not aggressive and do not play silly games;
- allow the candidate to do most of the talking;
- do not let personal prejudices interfere with their judgement;
- avoid future misunderstandings and dissatisfaction by being honest with the candidate and making sure that any disadvantages of the job are clearly understood;
- give the candidate a date for a decision and stick to it;
- do not make hasty decisions before all the candidates have been seen;
- do not lose sight of the basic requirements while interviewing;
- are not swayed by an attractive personality into giving the job to someone who does not fulfil the requirements;
- do not always give the job to the best of a bad bunch, but investigate where the recruiting methods and job specification may have gone wrong and start again;
- keep an eye on how employees develop, and learn from their mistakes.

Unsuccessful interviewers:

- think they have nothing to learn;
- rely on instinct and intuition;
- do not prepare their interviews;
- are frightened/intimidated by strong candidates;
- antagonize the candidate by aggression or inadequacy;
- do not listen to what is said;
- do most of the talking;
- ask questions requiring yes/no answers;
- allow outside noise and interruptions;
- do not make adequate notes after each interview.

6

Variations on the Selection Interview

Although we tend to think of selection interviewing as a conversation between two people there are several variations on this theme, all of which have their advantages and disadvantages.

Panel interviews

The first variation is the panel interview, where candidates are interviewed by several people. These tend to be used by very large companies, by companies or organizations where group decisions and committee work are a noticeable feature, and by very small organizations where everybody is regarded as equally important and may want a say in what is going on.

Advantages

Panel interviews have some advantages:

(a) They allow people with different areas of expertise to question the candidate more closely than one general interviewer.

(b) They are collectively responsible for appointments, making it less likely that one person will be unreasonably held to blame if anything goes wrong.

(c) They reveal how well the candidate performs in the company of a group of quite senior people.

(d) There is less likelihood of one person's prejudices or tendency to interview in his/her own likeness affecting the outcome.

Disadvantages

However, the disadvantages far outweigh the advantages:

(a) A major difficulty is getting all the appropriate people to be available at the required time, which may well run to several days if there are a lot of candidates.

(b) Because it is difficult to get everyone together, too little time and consideration will be given to making the final decision, which may well be made simply to bring the meeting to a close because one or other member of the panel has to get away.

(c) At its worst extreme, and particularly where the panel is a voluntary committee, all of whom are giving their time for nothing, the selection may well be made *without* all the panel having interviewed the candidate. This makes a mockery of the idea that panel interviews ensure a wide range of expertise. It also opens the way for acrimony and blame if the selected candidate is a failure.

(d) The more people on the panel, the more expensive the whole process becomes.

(e) A panel requires a very skilled chairman. This person will have to ensure that all members of the panel have seen and considered the candidates' original application forms and formulated questions arising from it. The chairman will also have to organize the panel during the interview, making sure that everyone has sufficient time to ask their questions but without allowing the process to get out of hand and overrun. Unfortunately skilled chairmanship is a rare gift. Poor chairmen may do all the talking, keep to a rigid schedule which prevents flexibility, or be unable to control the other members of the panel.

(f) A badly run panel interview will alienate the very people it is hoping to recruit as highly qualified and confident candidates are more than likely to be antagonized by a poor interview situation.

(g) Although a panel interview ensures that one person's particular prejudices do not overshadow the entire selection procedure, if all the people on the panel share the same prejudices then these will be reinforced. There is also the chance that everybody's prejudices will be brought to the situation. If there are enough of these then agreeing on a candidate may prove difficult, leaving the panel wide open to the danger of selecting the one candidate none of them feels strongly about rather than the best person for the job.

(h) Where a panel is composed of just two people a direct rivalry may spring up about who is in charge. If the interviewers find cooperation difficult the selection procedure will be very inefficient.

(i) Panel interviews are very intimidating for some interviewees who feel outnumbered and have a strong sense of 'me against all of them'. This results in unnecessarily poor interview performances in which the interviewers will not get an accurate picture of the candidates and their abilities.

(j) The last major disadvantage of panel interviews is that the interviewers may be more concerned with their relationship with each other than with relating to the candidate. They may be intent on impressing each other or the chairman or involved in little power games to prove who is the real leader of the group. This may manifest itself as verbal fireworks, overt pushiness or in one or other going for the 'wise elder statesman' role implying that she/he is the real source of any decision. It is very difficult for candidates to cope with all these nuances and to give an accurate picture of themselves. As a result, the panel actually gets in the way of discovering the very information it is there to find out.

Avoiding the pitfalls of panel interviews

If a panel interview is unavoidable, you can make it more efficient by:

(a) planning meetings and interviews well in advance so that members can all be available at the same time. This includes arranging time for discussion of the job/personnel specification beforehand, time for making a joint preliminary selection from application forms/c.v.s, and time for the decision-making meeting afterwards;

(b) involving the entire panel in drawing up the job/personnel specifications, wording the advertisement and deciding where it should be placed;

(c) drawing up a list of questions in advance, as advised for standard interviews, so that comparison between candidates is easier and the interviewers have a clear idea of what they are looking for;

(d) agreeing on interview timings in advance. This includes agreeing on the order in which different members of the panel will question the candidate and allotting the interview time between them;

(e) holding a 'dress rehearsal' beforehand so that the members of the panel can get used to working together rather than having to learn while the interview is in progress. This is particularly important where interview panels are made up of people who do not normally work together, and also where there are a lot of people who will take correspondingly longer to learn to work as a team.

In as many respects as possible the interview panel should try to follow the general interview format given in Chapter 5 (p. 94).

Sequential interviews

The second variation is the sequential interview. Many people think that this combines the good points of the one-to-one interview with those of the panel interview.

With this method all the people who wish to be involved in the selection of a candidate do so one after the other and not as one unwieldy group. They are able to ask questions and form opinions without being self-conscious about the other members of the selection group. They may have different areas of expertise and will be able to concentrate on these without having to sit through lengthy periods when colleagues are asking questions about their own area of interest.

There are three minor drawbacks. The candidates themselves may have to commit more time to the interview selection process; the interviewers will have to ensure they leave enough time for discussion between themselves as well as making their own post-interview notes; time will have to be set aside for the interviewers to meet and finalize their decision.

If these points can be arranged satisfactorily then the sequential interview is by far the most streamlined and efficient way of allowing more than one person to be involved in selection.

Tests and group interviews

As part of the selection process some interviewers and interview boards use group selection methods. These include residential interviews, workshops, discussions, group projects and psychological/intelligence tests. Such methods are outside the scope of this book, but those who are interested in reading more about them will find relevant books in Suggested Reading on p. 141. Several organizations run such courses and also teach their methods (see pp. 144–146).

PART III

Other Types of Interview

7

Interviews with Professionals

Getting a fair deal

Meeting with professionals such as doctors, accountants, lawyers, counsellors and bank managers can present problems even to the most articulate and outwardly confident people. These consultations are to all intents and purposes interviews, and should be treated as such. One of the reasons they are often confusing and unsatisfactory is that it is not always totally clear who is interviewing whom. You want advice, help, diagnosis, money, or any number of other things, and you should be in command of the situation in order to get exactly what you want out of it. The person from whom you have to get these things needs to interview you simultaneously in order to get the facts on which to base a judgement of what you need and/or whether you should have it. Because they are experts and you are not it is easy for them to take the initiative. As a result far too many people emerge from their doctor, lawyer or bank manager feeling that they have not had a fair deal and have been treated as children rather than as adults who know their own mind. Worst of all they leave without what they came for. There may be some justification for this if you are trying to explain away your overdraft to the bank manager yet again. There is no justification at all if you are asking for advice, arranging a loan, seeking help and advice from a doctor or paying a lawyer good money for his or her time.

Do not get a reputation for time-wasting

If you feel you often get unnecessarily short shrift in your interviews with professionals a question you must ask yourself is whether you have created an unfavourable impression by wasting their time in the past. Doctors encounter people who take up an undue amount of their time with trivial matters. Inevitably this affects their attitude to these people so that they tend to assume that all their visits are time-wasting. To a lesser extent bank managers and lawyers have the same problem. If you want to make the most out of your interviews with professional people, ensure that they will be prepared to take you seriously because they know you have not been a time-waster in the past.

Do not be timid

The opposite problem is experienced by those who are lacking in confidence, who feel that they should not worry other people with their problems and who, if they finally make an appointment, tend to rush through it and come away without covering all the points with which they had really hoped to deal.

There are several basic steps you can take to make yourself more effective in dealing with professionals of all kinds. Since in this situation you are both the interviewer and the candidate you can take advice from both the relevant sections of the book. The principles are the same—decide exactly what you want, do your preparation thoroughly, be confident.

Dealing with nervousness and stress

If much of your poor performance in these 'interviews' stems from nerves there are several positive steps you can take to help you become more relaxed (see pp. 39–44).

Decide what you want out of the interview

If you yourself do not know what you want out of the meeting you can hardly be surprised if the person you are dealing with does not respond in a satisfactory way.

Listing your objectives

The first thing you should do is write down clearly everything you want. Head a sheet of paper with the date and time of your meeting and make two columns, one for your essential objectives, the other of additional aims, which are desirable but not actually essential. This is not just a party trick. Actually formulating what you want and writing it down will clarify the situation amazingly in your mind, rather like trying to teach someone else something you have just learned.

For example, you might find when you come to make the list that all your objectives from a meeting with the doctor are essential such as 'appointment with specialist, something to alleviate symptoms, advice about unsightly scar on leg'. For a visit to the bank manager you might list as essential 'extending repayment period of loan' and

116

as desirable, 'explaining and reducing unreasonably high bank charges on last statement'.

Take plenty of time to work out your list and jot down every single thing you can think of.

Talk problems over beforehand

If appropriate, discuss the aims of your meeting with a friend, relative or colleague. Other people can often offer good ideas or may have useful experience from which you can benefit.

Be honest

By their very nature meetings with doctors, lawyers, bank managers and similar professionals can relate to very personal matters, problems which are sometimes hard to face up to. You will not get the best out of the professionals you consult unless you have a realistic appreciation of what you want and intend to be open and honest enough with them to give them the facts they will need to help you.

Draw up a list of questions

When you have noted down every single thing which you wish to discuss use the information to prepare a well-ordered list of questions to take in with you. *This is absolutely essential.* If you neglect to do this the chances are you will come away from the meeting having failed to raise several of the topics you wanted to deal with. It is much easier to work your way through a list, particularly if you are dealing with things that may embarrass or upset you, than it is to try and create order out of a general conversation. The person you are dealing with will also find it far easier to be helpful if she/he is clear about what the problem is and what you want. If you seem to be well organized and in command of the situation then you are likely to get an equally efficient response.

Remember—your list of questions should leave plenty of room for writing down the answers you get (do not forget to take a pen!).

Prepare all the facts and make them available

Inevitably you will have to present your accountant, doctor, lawyer, bank manager or counsellor with the information they will need in order to help you. Go to the meeting with all facts well researched and clearly written down. Facts are usually presented most simply and clearly in chronological order. (This will be easier if you have got into the habit of keeping a simple appointments diary.)

Take any relevant documents

Relevant bills and documents should be produced at the meeting, if they are available.

If you will need to relate what someone said or did take time beforehand to remember it clearly and note it down.

Ask for answers to be clarified

Take your time over your questions and any discussion which follows. Make sure you have fully understood what has been said to you. If in doubt ask the person to clarify it for you. Repeat what you think has been said so that any misunderstandings can be corrected.

If words or phrases are used which do not mean anything to you ask to have them explained to you in layman's terms. You should not need to feel inadequate because you do not understand all the technical terms of someone else's profession.

Do not be intimidated or distracted

Do not allow yourself to be intimidated. This may be easier said than done but if you have a clear idea of the purpose of the meeting and have prepared a thorough list of everything you want to know then you must stick to your guns and carry on relentlessly until you have worked your way through it.

Do not worry about the person who is coming after you. Once you have started your own meeting you should concentrate solely on yourself and what you want and not be distracted.

Being prepared for your meeting will save time and therefore, in many cases, money. Solicitors and private doctors charge a set rate for their time so use it economically.

Preparation will also enable you to get the best possible 'value' out of the expertise of the professional you are consulting who will have access to all the relevant facts and will be quite clear about what you are hoping to find out.

Additional points for consultation with your doctor

As well as defining what you want and making a list of questions there are several additional steps you can take to ensure you get the best possible results from your appointment with a general practitioner.

(a) Make a separate appointment for every person who is to see the doctor. Do not turn up with an extra child to be fitted in to the same appointment. Being inconsiderate to the doctor and other patients will get you off on a bad footing.

(b) Wear clothes which are easily taken off and put on if you think the doctor will want to examine you.

(c) Make a note of your problem, and the symptoms you associate with it, including when they started/got worse.

(d) Note down any other changes you may have noticed about yourself, even minor ones—you may not see the connection but they may be vital clues to the doctor.

(e) Keep a note of medicines or home treatments you have already tried and what effects, if any, they have had.

(f) Tell the doctor if you are allergic to anything, particularly any medicines.

(g) Tell the doctor if any close relatives have ever had similar problems.

(h) Women should make a note of the date of their last period.

Be honest

Honesty in answering the doctor's questions is particularly important. Do not cover up aspects of your lifestyle, such as heavy drinking, which you think may make you look less respectable. Most doctors are fairly unshockable, and they will need *all* the facts if they are to make a proper diagnosis.

Extra questions to add to your list

At the conclusion of the meeting there will probably be three questions you will need to ask and which should come at the end of your own list.

(a) The name of your illness or condition (if the doctor has reached any definite conclusions). Doctors do not always impart this information clearly to their patients.

(b) How to take your medicine (if any is prescribed). This includes knowing what time of day to take it, how long you should continue taking it (just until you feel better or until the end of the full course?), whether or not it has any side-effects (such as drowsiness), and whether or not it should not be taken in conjunction with certain foods or alcohol.

(c) Does the doctor wish to see you again, and if so, when?

Make sure the answers to these, as well as any other questions on your list, have been clearly noted.

Additional points for interviews with solicitors

Choosing a solicitor

Not all solicitors are good solicitors, some are incompetent, lazy and disorganized. Fortunately others are excellent and your aim initially is to find one of the good ones.

Ways of ensuring you find a good solicitor include:

(a) personal recommendation by someone whose opinion you respect;

(b) forming an opinion of the solicitor's office. Your business will be better handled by an efficient, well-organized, calm office than by one where the impression is one of barely contained chaos;

(c) a busy solicitor is usually a good solicitor;

(d) finding someone who specializes in your problem. Most firms have people with different areas of expertise. Some firms deal in one particular area of law;

(e) do not be alarmed if you are passed on from your initial solicitor (perhaps the one who did your house conveyancing) to another. This usually means the firm is giving you the person who specializes in your type of work, and this is a good sign.

When to change your solicitor

You are free to change your solicitor at any time and should do so if you feel your case is not being handled as you like. But remember that if you keep doing so you will find people are reluctant to take on your case. If you are dealing with a matter which upsets you, you may not be as objective in your judgement as you would normally be and you may be oversensitive. Try to take this into account when coming to a decision.

You should certainly change if:

(a) the solicitor has an existing client or an interest of his/her own which would prevent him/her from working solely in your interests. (Any reputable solicitor will declare this immediately so that you can take your case elsewhere.);

(b) you are not dealt with sympathetically (especially if it is a matter which is causing you emotional distress);

(c) there is evidence of incompetence (your file keeps getting lost!);

(d) the solicitor hurries you through the interview so that you feel you have not explained everything fully;

(e) you do not feel the solicitor has reached the heart of the problem. You can generally tell this by the sort of questions you are asked;

(f) you are not kept informed of events which happen as a result of the interview.

Time is money

Modern solicitors' offices are no longer run in a leisurely way. Clients are charged for the amount of time they take up, including the length of the interview and any telephone calls. This makes it all the more important to arrive at the interview well prepared. Bring a list of all the questions and queries you want answered, leaving plenty of room to make your notes. Bring all relevant documents.

When you are involved with other people (divorce or traffic accidents, for example) take ample time beforehand to think over your version of events and to write everything down.

Where relevant write down what you are aiming for (custody of the children, ownership of the house, damages for time off work, etc.). Do not wait until you are in the interview before formulating your aims.

A good solicitor will tell you if the expenses you are likely to incur (including the solicitors' own fees) will outweigh any financial benefit to be gained from your action. To be sure this point is covered, you should add it to your list of questions.

Become informed

Your attitude, especially if you are not accustomed to dealing with lawyers, will alter considerably if you familiarize yourself with the law as it affects you. A little background knowledge will make you more confident and help you to draw up a list of really relevant questions. The libraries are well stocked with books on the law, many of them designed to help the lay person. Some of the most straightforward of these are listed at the end of this book.

Additional points for interviews with bank managers

If the purpose of your interview is to raise finance, then your case will be helped immeasurably if you go into the interview with a clear and well-documented proposition.

Take business/personal details

This includes:

- details of your product or service;
- a brief history of your business, how/when it started.
- how it has developed:

or

- plans for a new business, including your reasons for setting it up, the relevant experience of those involved;
- information on the main people involved, including yourself. What is their expertise, experience, business experience;
- contingency plans if you or other main people involved are sick/absent;
- who are your main anticipated customers;
- who are your main competitors;
- any anticipated market developments.

Take financial details

You should also supply detailed financial information and details of finance you require. This includes:

- details of present debtors, creditors, stock and bank balance;
- details of financial commitments, including loans, overdrafts, leasing, hire purchase;
- bank statements for the last twelve months if you are applying to a bank other than your own;
- recent audited accounts (or equivalent);
- details of amount required, what it would be used for;
- how long you would require it;
- details of projected expenditure. Do not forget hidden costs like legal fees;
- do you anticipate further loans and/or an overdraft? If so, over what period?
- cash flow projection for at least three months (blank cash flow

forms are available at banks), including anticipated seasonal variations;

- details of any assets which could be offered as security (such as house, shares).

Although a loan may be important to you, do not forget that banks make their money by providing loans. They are not simply doing you a favour.

Useful books

Books with further advice on dealing with professionals are included in Suggested Reading. They include information on how to proceed if you are dissatisfied with the way a lawyer has handled your case or the diagnosis/treatment given by a doctor.

8

Interviews for University and College

Just as there is no certainty that however well prepared you are you will get the job for which you are being interviewed, there is no positive formula you can follow in order to be successful in an academic interview. However, there are some steps you can take to ensure you will stand out to the best possible advantage.

The basic interview technique applies

Much of the advice given to candidates for job interviews applies equally well to academic interviews, particularly the section on:

(a) coping with nerves and stress;
(b) filling in relevant forms as well as possible;
(c) anticipating questions so you will not be left with nothing to say;
(d) having good explanations for areas of poor performance;
(e) revising any academic or technical areas of knowledge you think you may be questioned on.

You should also look at the section on panel interviews as, given the communal nature of these places, you will probably have at least one interview with a group of people.

The interviewers want you to do well

An important point to be aware of is that few, if any, of the people you are going to meet will be hostile to you. You have been called to interview because of a good academic record and the dons or lecturers who interview you will be hoping that you will perform equally well at interview. They will be wanting:

(a) to put a face to the name on the form;
(b) to see whether you perform as well verbally and under cross-questioning as you do in the more straightforward academic tests of school and examination;
(c) to judge whether or not you are a social enough animal to cope with the pressures of communal university living (so make sure

124

at least some of the extracurricular activities you list are sociable);

(d) to decide if you can be self-motivated and organized without the benefit of a structured school day;

(e) to decide whether you have something extra to contribute apart from academic ability.

Different interviewers will have different priorities. You cannot anticipate all of them, nor can you adapt yourself instantly during an interview to fulfil all the expectations of several different people. However, you should be aware of the different approaches you may come across.

Interviews which stress academic ability

Academic interviewers fall into two main categories. The first group has a very straightforward approach, which emphasizes academic ability. With this type of interviewer, it is vitally important not to blunder into generalizations you cannot explain or back up with facts. Linguists may be given an 'unseen' to translate and be interviewed in the language they hope to study, scientists may be given a technical problem for which they must suggest solutions, historians may be required to account for historic events or movements or detect underlying trends in apparently unrelated events, law students may be given a case study to read and comment on. Since this is a highly likely eventuality it is worth taking plenty of time to revise any topics which you think may come up.

But do not prepare answers off by heart, especially if it is the received knowledge of your teacher or of one particular author.

Interviews which stress overall performance

Other university interviewers lay less stress on checking your academic and technical knowledge, which they feel that exam results have already amply indicated, and more on the way in which candidates respond to the cut and thrust of debate. They respond well to signs of original thinking. This can be very stimulating, and quite a revelation after school methods of study.

You may have found favour with your teacher by sitting quietly, taking everything in and reproducing it efficiently. At university level your interviewers will be looking for originality and signs that you are more than just an efficient sponge.

The danger in this situation is that it will turn into fireworks with no firm base. Be on your guard not to get carried away by the sound of your own voice and the flattering feeling of being treated as an equal or you may end up talking nonsense or talking for far too long.

However, since you will be judged on your ability to explain and defend any opinions, do not let politeness prevent you from replying to criticism of your arguments, as long as you are fairly sure of your ground.

Spend some time before the interview reading around your subject and trying to take a broader approach than you usually need for school and examinations. Make a conscious effort to come up with some thoughts and theories of your own (as long as you can justify them!), rather than rehearsing ideas you have picked up from a textbook. It will stand you in good stead if you have read books other than those on the syllabus or the ones that are your basic textbooks. Do not claim to have read books if you have not—you will be quickly found out.

Dons/lecturers who favour the second approach may well choose to discuss topics which are not directly within your scope, since they are concerned with your overall performance rather than your academic knowledge. It is a very good idea to keep up with current affairs before an interview, to have followed the major stories, to formulate some opinions about what is going on and have facts at your fingertips to back you up in a discussion.

Be prepared too for provocative questions such as, 'Why should a tax payer pay for you to come here?'—this is particularly popular if you are applying to study something unusual or with no obvious application.

Avoid being over-familiar

Academic interviews tend to have a more relaxed and informal feel than job selection interviews. But take care that the novelty of the experience does not lead you into over-familiarity, which can alienate people very fast indeed.

Presentation

It is also better not to be too casual in your approach to the matter of dress and presentation. The young executive look may not be necessary, but do your interviewers the courtesy of looking clean and tidy. After all among other things they will be trying to judge how you will manage to look after yourself when you are living away from home for what is probably the first time in your life. You will not be very convincing if you look as if you cannot get yourself organised even with all the back-up facilities of home.

9

Radio and Television
Interviews

Television and radio have lost much of their power to overawe over the last twenty years. While jobs in the media are still sought after and there is a certain amount of kudos to be gained from being on radio and television, both are much more accessible than they have ever been. It is quite likely that in one capacity or another you, or someone you know, will be involved in a radio or TV interview. This is partly because local radio and television have given more opportunities to career broadcasters, to local freelance contributors and to people who wish to air their opinions about matters of local interest and concern.

The interviewee

You are more likely to be involved with radio and (to a lesser extent) television as an interviewee rather than as an interviewer. With so many broadcasting hours to fill there is great scope for people who are involved in local projects, particularly fund-raising or campaigning on a matter of local concern and interest. Publicity will be useful for your cause and it will be an interesting experience. A little forward planning can take much of the anxiety out of the interview and help you make the most of your airtime.

Programme makers welcome good ideas

Clearly the first thing you must do is fix the interview. You may be approached directly by the radio or television station wanting to know more about your cause (or even wanting you to defend it). However, the chances are that you will need to make the first approach yourself as part of a general publicity campaign. Do not be shy about this. Programme makers have the constant anxiety of filling their time with subjects that are of interest to their listeners and viewers and they welcome ideas if they are well thought out, are of genuine interest and do not come from people who have lost their credibility by nagging them too often with silly or uninteresting ideas.

Since a lot of material arrives on the producer's desk every day, particularly on the news desk, you must make sure that your ideas stand out by being well presented and clearly of interest. With a news item this means writing a press release which sums up the points you are hoping to put across, gives information about the time, date and nature of the particular event (if any) which you are arranging, emphasizes how the project is of genuine interest to an audience, states clearly who should be contacted and gives a telephone number where someone will be available.

Is it visual?

When working out where to send your press release, bear in mind that most items for television have to have a visual content. Radio is much more versatile because interest is created purely out of what can be heard. Television does do straightforward interviews but if there is nothing to see your idea will have to be very strong, or of considerable local interest. If your subject is the demolition of buildings of local and historical interest, possibly with a demonstration against it, then the news editor will be able to envisage some interesting pictures. If your concern is with the nitrate content of lettuces being sold in the local shops this will not be an immediately visual subject and you might do better to concentrate your energies on getting interviewed on the radio.

Prepare your facts

If you are going to be interviewed on either radio or television, then you should follow the golden rule for all interviews and be prepared. Do not expect to be able to make it up as you go along, even if you are normally a very fluent speaker among your friends. Being broadcast has a nasty habit of making even the most self-assured person suddenly dry up at the thought of all those people out there. So make sure you have a thorough grasp of your subject.

Have ready answers for awkward questions

As with any interview you should be particularly prepared for the awkward questions. There will be more of these than in a job selection interview as the interviewer has been taught that provocative questions produce more interesting answers than those requiring straightforward explanations. If you are being interviewed because of a controversial matter, for example you want to site a smelly factory next to a local park, then you would be naive to expect anything other than awkward questions. You will get more sympathetic treatment if you are raising money for the local hospice, but even so the interviewer may choose to put forward the objections of those who do not support you.

Use notes but not prepared speeches

It is very important to keep talking, particularly if you are being attacked. Sudden silence may be regarded as admission of defeat. However, you should not prepare full written answers to possible questions as it will not be possible to read them out on television, and even on radio they have a very false feel to them, particularly, strangely enough, if you are trying to be amusing. However, it is a good idea to make out cards for yourself with a few key points, to jog your memory about the topics you would like to cover, or as a note of key facts and figures which might easily go out of your head. If you appear several times on television or radio you will become more relaxed about the entire experience, and you may find notes entirely unnecessary to you, but they contribute wonderfully to your confidence the first time around.

Practise with a tape-recorder

Another piece of advice from job selection interviews which is equally appropriate to broadcasting interviews, is to practise hearing the sound of your own voice beforehand. If you are hoping to earn money for your broadcasts, even as a very occasional freelance, you have probably already practised with a tape-recorder. If you are simply representing a cause or an organization ask a friend or colleague to 'interview' you for a few minutes while the tape-recorder is running, or just practise by yourself saying what you want to say into a tape-recorder. When you listen back you will be able to judge whether or not there are too many 'ums' and 'ers' and whether you say what you have to say as clearly and efficiently as possible.

Interviews are usually very short

Although it is vital to have thought before the interview about what you want to say and the overall message you are trying to put across, a common mistake with first-time interviewees is to overestimate the amount of time at their disposal, and to come armed with too much information. Few interviews, on radio *or* television, last more than three minutes. Most last considerably less, as it is assumed that viewers/listeners have only a very limited length of concentration.

Be prepared to give the fundamental points of what you want to say in a concise fashion. Detail will only be required for in-depth interviews which are few and far between. Do not make the very basic mistake of presenting only a fraction of what you wanted to say because you thought you would get the opportunity to speak at leisure.

Dealing with nervousness

It is quite common to be a little bit nervous—even the great and good feel nervous. Basically it's because you want to be liked. Hollywood veteran Katharine Hepburn remarked recently, 'I'm nervous about interviews. I just hope I'll be interesting—just the way you're nervous wondering if someone will dance with you at the age of 15 at parties.'

There is some useful advice on controlling and overcoming nervousness in Part I (pp. 39–44). Relaxation is important because you will then be in command of your situation even if much of the technical side of what is happening is unfamiliar to you.

The very best advice is *be yourself*. Once you forget about trying to adapt yourself, your personality and what you have to say to what suits the interviewer, a lot of the tension will disappear.

Control irritating mannerisms

One of the side-effects of stress is that it tends to bring out any nervous mannerisms you may have. Your hands may start flapping in the most affected way. Your foot may tap up and down, you may flick your fingers constantly. Not surprisingly these mannerisms can alienate people so much they may not even listen to what you have to say. Try to control irritating mannerisms particularly if you are being interviewed on television. If you can take criticism, ask a friend to point them out to you so that you are forewarned.

Let the interviewer do the worrying

If the interviewer seems more terrified than you are (and a lot of them are!) forget it, it's not your problem. Nor is it your problem to see that the item comes out on time. Be courteous and considerate. Try to make your answers precise. Do not ramble so that it is difficult to bring the interview to a neat conclusion or move on to another topic, but do not take on yourself the burden of seeing that it goes well. That is outside your scope and thinking about it will make it difficult for you to do yourself justice.

Do not react to aggressive interviewing

If the interviewer tries to annoy or upset you do not allow yourself to be pushed into retaliation. Your overall manner and the way you handle an issue will be remembered long after the precise details which you may have fought to say are forgotten.

Sincerity and honesty will show

Another approach which will make you more effective is to be honest. It is a cliché that radio, and television in particular, show up liars and phonies, but on the whole it is true. Sincerity and honesty come over clearly, and if you cannot lay claim to those particular qualities on certain topics it might be better not to do yourself the bad turn of saying your piece in public.

Do not use unfamiliar jargon

It is also important to avoid using jargon, abbreviations, or initials which may be meaningful to others in the same field as yourself but which do not mean a thing to the majority of people who are listening to you. If technical language is essential explain it yourself (work out a simple definition in advance).

Make it interesting

Do not talk in a very abstract way. Giving examples and drawing visual pictures will make what you have to say much more interesting, and people may listen rather than get up to make the tea while you are on. Do not be patronising and talk down to your audience, even if you are trying to 'educate' people.

Be conversational not declamatory

Do be conversational in the way that you talk. Queen Victoria once complained that Prime Minister Gladstone addressed her as though she were a public meeting. If you do that to your audience you too will get a negative response. You may find yourself in an unfamiliar situation behind a microphone, possibly with cameras peering at you, but the viewers and listeners will be in the familiar surroundings of their own homes, and will react badly if you do not behave as if you are actually there talking with them.

Learn by studying others

If you know you are going to be interviewed for radio or television, or if you are going to do a broadcast of your own, it is sensible to study others who are in the same line of work. Decide who you think are particularly effective, try to analyse why they are successful. Are they relaxed, friendly, good at presenting complicated information simply, do they smile a lot, really listen and respond to the people they talk to, seem unaffected and not to be putting on an act? Watch other people being interviewed, decide what is good about them and where they fail and try to put what you observe into practice.

These may seem a lot of do's and don'ts for a newcomer to being interviewed, but if you learn the basic rules the chances are you will get asked back again. Producers always like to have articulate cooperative people with their own areas of expertise on whom they can call.

Some people have even started full-time careers in broadcasting by being good interviewees.

What happens on location or in the studio

It is useful to know approximately what to expect if an interviewer comes to your home or if you go to a radio or television studio.

There will probably first be some discussion of what the interview will contain. If you want to, and you are talking about something which makes you feel very threatened, you can insist that you see all the questions beforehand and veto those you do not like. However, it will get you off on a bad footing and it may be better to refuse an interview altogether than to give one in which you require such stringent control.

What you can reasonably expect is that the interviewer will give you a rough idea of the ideas she/he expects to cover. This gives you an opportunity to mention anything you also are keen to include. You will be told the length of time the interview will run, so that you can judge the length of your answers (in order to cover as much as possible in the time) and what sort of people will be listening— whether it will be a general audience or one with an expert knowledge and interest in the topic.

Do not regard talking things over as the opportunity to do a full-scale rehearsal or you will lose spontaneity when the time comes to do it for real. Just state briefly the topics you will be covering. If you are being interviewed because of your expertise—for example, you may know what makes a certain scientific process work or how to operate an interesting machine—the interviewer may actually give you a brief plan of what is wanted and ask you to go over what you will say to judge whether or not you are being clear enough. If it is a television interview and certain shots are planned to back up your explanation you may be asked to do things in a certain order. By all means try to do what is wanted but do remember that ultimately it is the experts' job to make it work; do not allow worry about doing it properly to spoil your own performance.

If you are at home do not be surprised or irritated if the curtains are drawn and/or furniture is moved to help the sound quality. The telephone may be taken off the hook or anything making a continuous sound such as a clock or noisy central heating may be turned off. The sound person or reporter will want to cut background noise to a minimum so that if the interview is cut or edited there will be no strange jumps where the background does not match.

Leave yourself plenty of time for television interviews

If the interview is taking place in a studio you will be given a definite time to turn up. With a radio interview you will generally find that you are in and out in about the time you would expect. Television interviews, unless they go out live, in which case there is much less time for messing around, generally seem to take up a lot more time. This is mainly because technically they are much more complicated. Anyway it is a good idea to turn up expecting to take a long time.

Studio personnel

In a radio studio there will probably be just you and the interviewer with an engineer visible through a glass partition, who does most of the technical work.

In the television studio will be an amazing number of people milling around, with a director in overall charge up in the 'box' and a floor manager to keep things organized and liaise between the director and everyone on the studio floor.

Voice level tests

In every case, whether in a studio or on location you will be asked to do a short voice test for level. Try and be relaxed about this and speak as you will do once things get going. Do not try to speak in anything other than your normal voice. The sound engineer will make the necessary adjustments, but will be understandably annoyed if after altering the controls to suit what appears to be your normal voice she/he finds that something quite different is emerging once the interview starts for real. If your mind goes a blank when asked for a voice level, try telling them what you had for breakfast, how you travelled to the studio or even a joke.

Appearance

The joy of radio is that it does not matter what you look like, although strangely enough you perform better if you think that you are looking all right. Television imposes certain restraints, which is one of the reasons why relaxing is so much more difficult on television. The best advice is to wear something in which you feel comfortable but which will not insult the viewer by looking as though you could not be bothered to take any trouble. You should not wear clothes which are covered in small dots or stripes as these seem to join up when the camera is on them and create a strange glare (strobing). Large expanses of plain bright white can be a problem (not if it is just a collar or a glimpse of a shirt). So too can fabrics like silk, which rustle.

In television, personal microphones are usually pinned somewhere on your clothes. This can be a real problem because the rustle is greatly magnified by the proximity of the sensitive microphone and sounds something akin to Niagara Falls. Noel Coward once remarked to a sound engineer who was wrestling to overcome the problems presented by his expensive silk tie, 'Is my tie too loud for you, dear boy?'

Another sound problem to beware of is gesticulating and either covering or bumping your microphone. This will cause your voice to fade or strange bumps and clicks to intersperse what you are saying. It is a particular problem with inexperienced interviewees who sometimes resort to nervous gestures such as straightening their tie.

A very minor tip, but one which may save you some embarrassment, is to eat something beforehand, even if you are nervous. Otherwise the microphone pinned to your person may well pick up the sounds of your tummy rumbling!

These considerations are not so important in radio where personal microphones are rarely used.

After the interview

When the interview is over do not expect to linger. If you are in a radio studio you will be whisked out as soon as your time is up. In a television studio you may get a chance to remove your make up, but unless you are a particularly significant person there will not be

much of the fabled hospitality. Just make yourself pleasant, hope it
went well and with any luck you'll be asked back another time.

The interviewer

Learning to be a professional interviewer is almost entirely a matter
of experience. Unless you go to a college where broadcasting
techniques are taught you will learn the tricks of the trade as you go
along, from other interviewers, from helpful or exasperated
directors, from other technicians and from your own common
sense. However, in this section we have included some useful hints
which may stop you making too many elementary errors when you
start out. These should also be useful to people making programme
inserts for local radio on behalf of pressure groups and people who
want to make occasional freelance contributions on subjects which
are of particular interest to them.

The ideal interviewer:

(a) is relaxed, able to make the interviewees feel at ease and
ready to talk in his or her company;
(b) has mastered what the interview is about (even if the whole
thing is forgotten the minute the interviewee has gone);
(c) leaves interviewees feeling happy that they had the opportunity to say what they wanted to say.

Being a radio or television interviewer is not for you:

(a) if you are so paralysed with fright you are dominated by your
interviewee;
(b) if you have to be aggressive;
(c) if you cannot actually listen and respond to what is said;
(d) if, even after some practice, your idea of a nightmare is an
interviewee who is spontaneous and ready for a real give-and-
take conversation rather than an awkward prearranged
exchange.

Get to know the interviewee

Always give yourself enough time to speak to the interviewee
before you begin, even if it is only during the short period while the
interview is being set up. If you are doing a live radio show, when
the guests will arrive and depart while the show is on the air, then
telephone the day before to introduce yourself and talk about what
you are going to say. Unless you are looking for hard-hitting

political debate (and possibly even then), you will get much more out of an interviewee who regards you as a friend.

Discuss the content and shape of the interview

You should talk over the length of time of the interview, what the interviewee wants to say, what you also would like to come out of the conversation, and possibly the order of the questions if they have to give a voice-over for film of some specific occurrence or process.

Do not rehearse the questions in detail or, the next time round, when it really matters, it will sound stale. Worse still, the interviewee may subconsciously feel she/he cannot repeat what has already been said because under normal circumstances that would be very boring for you!

Some interviewees prefer to go straight into an interview without any discussion as they feel they give a more natural performance that way. On radio, unless the show goes out live and you are not confident you can handle it, why not let them? After all it is usually easy to cut and edit a radio interview. With television you have to be a little more sure of your ability to handle a completely unexpected conversation as re-recording and editing are expensive and the director will prefer to avoid it if at all possible.

Do your background research

A little background research is important if you are to be really confident you can handle everything which comes out of the interview. It is also a courtesy to the person you are interviewing. Few people react well to an interview which begins, 'I haven't actually read your book but . . .' If you have done some research you will already have an idea of what you want to say before you meet/talk to the interviewee and you can have noted some possible questions which you think would make a logical progression through the subject. The longer the interview obviously the more research you will require.

Really listen to what is said

Even though it is a good idea to have some prepared questions you should really listen to the interviewee as the interview progresses. Too many interviewers (probably as a result of nerves) simply stare glassily at their guest without taking in a word of what has been said. They then turn with relief to the next question on the list without following up a potentially interesting point or digression which has been made. If you really listen and respond you will get a much more lively and informative interview. It is more difficult and more nerve-racking but it is more professional, and much more interesting for the audience, which may well be irritated at an interviewer's persistent failure to follow up an interesting development.

Nerves

Interviewers, as well as interviewees, get nervous, and this is a major reason why many of them become boring. If you are nervous you regard the interview as an ordeal to be got through and not as an interesting conversation you are having on behalf of the viewers or listeners. Also if you are nervous you will not be very successful at putting the guest at ease. There are some hints for overcoming nervousness on p. 39. Many interviewers, particularly television interviewers (television is more demanding and creates more tension), are nervous every time they perform. A little adrenaline is probably a good thing and keeps you on your toes, but if you find you are taking pills or alcohol to calm you down then you are in the wrong job.

Do not antagonize the interviewee

You should always be calm and courteous; it is your job to put your guest at ease. There is never any reason or excuse for antagonizing a guest.

Background information is not part of the interview

Background information should be given by the presenter or even yourself, before the interview starts. It should not usually be part of the interview. Ask the main questions early in the interview, especially if it is a short news item.

Questions: what not to do

Do not ask questions that can be answered with a straight 'yes' or 'no'. Do not answer the questions yourself as you ask them. For example, 'I expect watching your car roll over the edge of the cliff was rather a nasty experience for you, wasn't it?' What can the interviewee say except 'yes'. It is far better to start as many questions as possible with how, why, when, where, what and which; for instance, you might say, 'How did you react when you saw the car start to move?', or 'What did you do when you saw the car start to move?' Either way you will get a more interesting answer.

Soft-pedal your own personality

Although your interview will be most successful if it is conversational in tone, do not forget that it is the interviewee the audience wants to hear, not you. Some of the most annoying interviewers are those who insist on giving us the benefit of their personality rather than helping to get the best out of the interviewee.

Keep quiet while your interviewee is talking

Try not to interrupt. Do not come in with your own witty remarks to top those of your guest. Do not punctuate the conversation with little encouraging grunts and remarks like 'Oh really', or even worse (and this happens a lot in private conversations) finishing off the interviewee's sentences for them or chiming in with their words as they come to the end of a sentence. A good interview should feel like a conversation, but it should be a controlled conversation in which the interviewer plays the role of sympathetic listener and prompt rather than that of the primary figure.

Silent encouragement

If you want to encourage the interviewee to keep going then nod, smile encouragingly or give a sympathetic or encouraging look to your face. Just keep it silent, even on television. Although you may feel that in television encouraging noises will seem natural because you can be seen, remember that for a lot of the time the camera has only got the interviewee in shot and conversational noises will sound just as strange and disembodied as they do on the radio.

Assess your performance during the interview

Try and get into the habit of continuously assessing your own performance as you go along. Are you helping the interviewee to relax? Are you keeping to the subject? Are you making sure you will be through in the allotted time? Are you really listening and responding? Are you avoiding irritating mannerisms?

Location radio interviews

If you are going out to do radio interviews you should be given the basic technical knowledge by whoever has commissioned you. However, it is easy to forget this, and you may want to try some interviews independently, without the benefit of anyone else's advice. There are a few simple rules which will help you come up with a professional sounding interview.

(a) You must use equipment which is of a good enough technical standard. Check with whoever you are hoping to sell the interview to about which sort of equipment will give adequate reproduction. If they are really interested in your idea they may lend you a professional machine like a Uher.

(b) Have an approximate interview structure in mind and have some questions ready prepared.

(c) Your interview will be more saleable if it is the right length. In general, aim for between two and three minutes' finished length unless you have been asked for anything different.

(d) It is relatively cheap and simple to edit radio tapes, so record a little more than that so you have some room for manoeuvre. You can also afford to let an interviewee ramble on a little longer than you could do if you were in the studio, and this may give you more interesting material to edit from than if you made the person stick to a set time.

(e) When asking questions, put yourself in the place of the listener. Would you understand what was being said if you had not already done some research? If not, get your interviewee to clarify.

(f) Make sure interviewees explain any technical or professional jargon.

(g) You will need to take a sound level before starting the interview.

(h) You should take any telephones off the hook so that you are not interrupted.

(i) If there is a noise such as aircraft or roadworks either wait for it to stop or move your location. It will be almost impossible for you to edit if there is a strong background noise as the cuts will be very obvious.

(j) Be aware of background noises in the room such as electric heaters. It is easy to overlook them when you are there, but they will come out very strongly on the tape. Switch them off if at all possible.

(k) If there are any noises which cannot be prevented then explain them to the listener who otherwise will be distracted and irritated by them.

(l) It is a good idea to draw the curtains in a room if there is any problem with extraneous noise, as this goes a long way to muffling it.

(m) Avoid rooms with very high ceilings which will give an echoing effect.

(n) Avoid rooms which are uncarpeted as this, too, can make it sound as though the interview is taking place in a barn.

Further reading for both interviewers and interviewees is given in Suggested Reading on p. 141. Pages 144–146 give addresses of organizations which specialize in teaching broadcasting techniques for people on both sides of the microphone.

Suggested Reading

The book list in this chapter is intended to give a wide range of further reading to people who are interested in all aspects of interviewing.

The interviewee

First-time job hunters

Applications and Interviews, AGCAS, Central Services Unit (available from University Careers Offices)

How to Succeed at an Interview and How to Survive if you Don't, Kris Box and Don Cole (EP Publishing Ltd, 1982)

Working It Out, Careers and Occupational Information Centre (available from COIC Sales Dept, Freepost, Sheffield, SL1 4BR)

How to be Interviewed, D. McKenzie Davey and P. McDonell (British Institute of Management Foundation, 1975)

Job Finding: A Step by Step Guide, Penny Hackett (John Murray, 1983)

How to Get a Job, Marjorie Harris (Institute of Personnel Management, 3rd edn, 1983)

Coping with Interviews, Martin Higham (New Opportunities Press, 1983)

The Job-finders' Book, Ruth Sandys and Alexa Stace (Kogan Page, 1979)

Kogan Page published a series called 'Careers in . . .' (land and property, psychology, banking, etc.) each of which have a chapter on the interview

Get that Job, Manpower Services Commission (leaflet available from Job Centres or MSC, Sheffield, S1 4PQ)

Mature job-hunters

Getting the Job you Want, Howard Dowding and Sheila Boyce (Ward Lock, 1979)

Changing Your Job after 35, Godfrey Golzen and Philip Plumbley (Kogan Page, 1984)

Get That Job, Ivan Hussell and John Kellett (Macdonald, 1982)

Coping with Redundancy, Fred Kemp, Bernard Butler and Derek Kemp (Hamlyn Paperbacks, 1981)

Successful Job Hunting, R. C. I. Miller (Basil Blackwell, 1983)

Back to Work—A Practical Guide for Women, Cathy Moulder and Pat Shelton (Kogan Page, 1979)

The Job Hunting Handbook, Professional and Executive Recruitment (a branch of the Manpower Services Commission, Sheffield, S1 4PQ)

The interviewer

Recruitment Techniques, Tina Agrell (Thorsons, 1977)

Introduction to Selection Interviewing, Edgar Anstey (HMSO, 1977)

How to Interview, D. McKenzie Davey and P. McDonell (British Institute of Management Foundation, 1980)

Employment Interviewing, John Munro Fraser (Macdonald and Evans, 1978)

How to Recruit and Select Successful Salesmen, John Lidstone (Gower, 1983)

Recruitment and Selection, Philip Plumbley (Institute of Personnel Management, 1968)

The Seven Point Plan, A. Rodger (National Institute of Industrial Psychology, 1951)

Selection Interviewing, Peter Whitaker (The Industrial Society, 1973)

Body language

Body Language, Allan Pease (Sheldon Press, 1984)

Interviews with professionals

Pre-interview Reference Books

Doctors and the Law, N. Leigh Taylor (Oyez/Longman in the It's Your Law Series, 1976)

A Patient's Guide to the National Health Service, Consumers' Association/Patients Association (Hodder and Stoughton, 1983)

Before You See a Solicitor, Gerald Sanctuary (Oyez/Longman in the It's Your Law Series, 1983). Further titles in this series include: *Accidents and the Law*, *Company Directors and the Law*, *Consumers—Know Your Rights*, *The Courts and You*, *Marriage and the Law*, *Motorists and the Law*, *Police and the Law*, *Your Business and the Law*, *Your Home and the Law*.

A Penguin Guide to the Law, John Pritchard (Penguin, 1982)

Problem-Solving Interviews, W. E. Beveridge (George Allen and Unwin, 1968)

Radio and television

A Guide to Broadcasting Techniques, Elwyn Evans (Barrie Jenkins, 1977)

Helpful Organizations

Government organizations

Manpower Services Commission, Sheffield S1 4PQ

Careers and Occupational Information Centre (part of the Manpower Services Commission), Moorfoot, Sheffield S1 4PQ. Produces a 'Working in . . .' series (hospitals, computers, engineering crafts), which are described as 'the next best thing to conducting a series of personal interviews'. These are available by post from either your local COIC Bookshop, or the above address

Jobclubs. There are now nearly 30, including those at Durham, Middlesbrough, Sunderland and Walthamstow. More are opening every month. Ask at your local job centre for details of your nearest one and how to join

Jobmate. National Extension College, 8 Strutton Ground, London SW1 2HP. Produces a free kit for Londoners under 21 (25 in Camden). Section 6 deals with interviews. They can also put you in touch with someone who knows your area of London and the problems you might encounter while job-hunting

Professional and Executive Recruitment (government employment agency, part of the Manpower Services Commission), Regent Street, London SW1Y 4PP. Run a weekly half-day seminar in job-hunting for people registered with PER through job centres. They also publish *Executive Post*, which lists vacancies, and is displayed in job centres and posted to members.

Evening institutes. Local authorities often run evening courses useful to interviewees and interviewers. Typical classes are, 'Confidence building and preparation for interview', 'Assertion training', 'Public speaking', 'Interviewing for writers and researchers', and 'Starting/running your own business'. Details are usually available from public libraries.

Non-government organizations

British Institute of Management, Management House, Cottingham Road, Corby, Northants NN17 1TT. Tel: 0536 204222.

They run courses (for members and non-members) on selection interviews, body language, and appraisal, which are most suitable for line managers and personnel specialists. Courses are for one–two days, or two weeks; prices are about £200 for members, £240 for non-members for short courses.

Institute of Personnel Management, IPM House, Camp Road, Wimbledon, London SW19 4UW. Tel: 01 946 9100.
The IPM Information Department Library has extensive reading lists covering recruitment and selection, group selection and the selection interview. Books and pamphlets are available on loan to IPM members. Copies of articles may also be purchased by non-members. The library also has lists of IPM publications available by post, and sample application forms.

The Industrial Society, Peter Runge House, 3 Carlton House Terrace, London SW1Y 5DG. Tel: 01 839 4300.
They run communication skills courses (including interviewing skills) for management, supervisors and other personnel staff. The one-to-three day courses cater for those with experience but no formal training as well as those with some knowledge of interviewing techniques. They are open to members and non-members of the IS, limited to 15 people, and cost about £235.

Marketing Improvements Ltd, Ulster House, Ulster Terrace, London NW1. Tel: 01 487 5811.
This company runs management workshops for small groups and lays great stress on the importance of selection interviewing.

Samurai course at the Actors' Institute
They hold a ten-week careers course, run from 7.00 am to 9.00 am two mornings a week. Not exclusively an 'interview' course, but built round the question, 'What next?' It works particularly with people's creativity—how you market yourself, how you can better express your creativity, how to strike out what you don't want. For further details write to the Course Manager, Gillian Edwards, Actors' Institute, 137 Goswell Road, London EC1V 7ET. Tel: 01 251 8178.

Radio and television courses

CTVC, Hillside Studios Ltd, Merry Hill Road, Bushey, Watford, WD2 1DR. Tel: 01 950 4426.
They run a variety of courses on radio and television (for

example, how broadcasting works and how to use it effectively), as well as personal presentation and religious/personal communication and courses tailormade to individual requirements. Course membership is usually restricted to eight people, and a two-day course costs £600 to non-church members.

Stanley Hyland, TV Consultant Advisor, HyVision Studios, 43 Earlham Street, London WC2. Tel: 01 836 6938.
This firm runs television sessions tailored to individual/company needs, but they might prove costly to non-sponsored individuals.

National Broadcasting School, 14 Greek Street, London, W1. Tel: 01 434 2411.
They run a three-month summer course with the Royal College of Art called 'Craft of TV Production', covering *all* aspects of television work—camera, lighting, interviewing, etc.

Video Image Projection, 154 Fleet Street, London, EC4. Tel: 01 583 0544.
They run 'communication in industry' courses to improve communications within and between industry for senior management who might be appearing on television and for evaluation of staff/head hunting. They also offer a service in video and satellite conferencing.

Application/c.v. forms

Printed application forms for job hunters (with career history forms printed on the back) to be filled in by candidates are available from: Search-Write Stationery Company, 28 Hale Close, Melbourn, Royston, Herts SG8 6ET. Tel 0763 61936.

Application forms for employers

These are available from the Institute of Personnel Management (see p. 145).